Lake Oswego Jr. High
2500 SW Country Club Rd.
Lake Oswego, OR 97034
503-534-2335

Reconstruction:
Life After the Civil War

THE
CIVIL WAR
A NATION DIVIDED

A NATION DIVIDED

Reconstruction:
Life After the Civil War

Tim McNeese

CHELSEA HOUSE
PUBLISHERS
An imprint of Infobase Publishing

RECONSTRUCTION: LIFE AFTER THE CIVIL WAR

Chelsea House
An imprint of Infobase Publishing
132 West 31st Street
New York NY 10001

Library of Congress Cataloging-in-Publication Data
McNeese, Tim.
  Reconstruction : life after the Civil War / by Tim McNeese.
      p. cm. — (The Civil War : a nation divided)
  Includes bibliographical references and index.
  ISBN 978-1-60413-035-5 (hardcover)
  1. Reconstruction (U.S. history, 1865-1877) I. Title. II. Series.

  E668.M158 2009
  973.8—dc22   2008026564

Chelsea House books are available at special discounts when purchased in bulk quantities for businesses, associations, institutions, or sales promotions. Please call our Special Sales Department in New York at (212) 967-8800 or (800) 322-8755.

You can find Chelsea House on the World Wide Web at
http://www.chelseahouse.com

Series design by Lina Farinella
Cover design by Keith Trego

Printed in the United States of America

Bang FOF 10 9 8 7 6 5 4 3 2 1

This book is printed on acid-free paper.

All links and Web addresses were checked and verified to be correct at the time of publication. Because of the dynamic nature of the Web, some addresses and links may have changed since publication and may no longer be valid.

Contents

Chronology

1820   The Missouri Compromise allows Maine to be admitted to the Union as a free state and Missouri as a slave state in 1821.

1831   William Lloyd Garrison publishes the first issue of the abolitionist newspaper, *The Liberator*.

1836   The House passes a gag rule that automatically tables or postponed action on all petitions relating to slavery without hearing them.

1838   The Underground Railroad is formally organized.

1845   Former slave Frederick Douglass publishes his autobiography, *Narrative of the Life of Frederick Douglass, An American Slave*.

1850   Congress enacts several measures that together make up the Compromise of 1850.

1852   Harriet Beecher Stowe publishes *Uncle Tom's Cabin*.

1854   Congress passes the Kansas-Nebraska Act, which overturns the Missouri Compromise and thus opens northern territories to slavery.

1855   As Kansas prepares to vote, thousands of Border Ruffians from Missouri enter the territory in an attempt to influence the elections. This begins the period known as Bleeding Kansas.

1856   South Carolina representative Preston Brooks attacks Massachusetts Senator Charles Sumner on the Senate floor and beats him with a cane.

1857   The Supreme Court rules, in *Dred Scott v. Sandford*, that blacks are not U.S. citizens and slaveholders have the right to take slaves into free areas of the country.

1859   John Brown seizes the arsenal at Harpers Ferry, Virginia. Robert E. Lee, then a Federal Army regular, leads the troops that capture Brown.

1860   **NOVEMBER**   Abraham Lincoln is elected president.

DECEMBER   A South Carolina convention passes an ordinance of secession, and the state secedes from the Union.

1861   **JANUARY**   Florida, Alabama, Georgia, and Louisiana secede from the Union.

FEBRUARY   Texas votes to secede from the Union. The Confederate States of America is formed and elects Jefferson Davis as its president.

MARCH   Abraham Lincoln is sworn in as the sixteenth president of the United States and delivers his first inaugural address.

APRIL 12   At 4:30 A.M., Confederate forces fire on South Carolina's Fort Sumter. The Civil War begins. Virginia secedes from the Union five days later.

MAY   Arkansas and North Carolina secede from the Union.

JUNE   Tennessee secedes from the Union.

JULY 21   The Union suffers a defeat in northern Virginia, at the First Battle of Bull Run (Manassas).

AUGUST   The Confederates win the Battle of Wilson's Creek, in Missouri.

1862   **FEBRUARY 6**   In Tennessee, Union general Ulysses S. Grant captures Fort Henry. Ten days later, he captures Fort Donelson.

MARCH   The Confederate ironclad ship CSS *Virginia* (formerly the USS *Merrimack*) battles the Union ironclad *Monitor* to a draw. The Union's Peninsular Campaign begins in Virginia.

APRIL 6-7   Ulysses S. Grant defeats Confederate forces in the Battle of Shiloh (Pittsburg Landing), in Tennessee.

APRIL 24   David Farragut moves his fleet of Union Navy vessels up the Mississippi River to take New Orleans.

MAY 31   The Battle of Seven Pines (Fair Oaks) takes place in Virginia.

JUNE 1   Robert E. Lee assumes command of the Army of Northern Virginia.

JUNE 25–JULY 1   The Seven Days Battles are fought in Virginia.

AUGUST 29–30   The Union is defeated at the Second Battle of Bull Run.

SEPTEMBER 17   The bloodiest day in U.S. military history: Confederate forces under Robert E. Lee are stopped at Antietam, Maryland, by Union forces under George B. McClellan.

SEPTEMBER 22   The first Emancipation Proclamation to free slaves in the rebellious states is issued by President Lincoln.

DECEMBER 13   The Union's Army of the Potomac, under Ambrose Burnside, suffers a costly defeat at Fredericksburg, Virginia.

1863   **JANUARY 1**   President Lincoln issues the final Emancipation Proclamation.

JANUARY 29   Ulysses S. Grant is placed in command of the Army of the West, with orders to capture Vicksburg, Mississippi.

MAY 1–4   Union forces under Joseph Hooker are defeated decisively by Robert E. Lee's much smaller forces at the Battle of Chancellorsville, in Virginia.

MAY 10   The South suffers a huge blow as General Thomas "Stonewall" Jackson dies from wounds he received during the battle of Chancellorsville.

JUNE 3   Robert E. Lee launches his second invasion of the North; he heads into Pennsylvania with 75,000 Confederate troops.

JULY 1–3   The tide of war turns against the South as the Confederates are defeated at the Battle of Gettysburg in Pennsylvania.

JULY 4   Vicksburg, the last Confederate stronghold on the Mississippi River, surrenders to Ulysses S. Grant after a six-week siege.

JULY 13–16   Antidraft riots rip through New York City.

JULY 18   The black 54th Massachusetts Infantry Regiment under Colonel Robert Gould Shaw assaults a fortified Confederate position at Fort Wagner, South Carolina.

SEPTEMBER 19–20   A decisive Confederate victory takes place at Chickamauga, Tennessee.

NOVEMBER 19   President Lincoln delivers the Gettysburg Address.

NOVEMBER 23–25   Ulysses S. Grant's Union forces win an important victory at the Battle of Chattanooga, in Tennessee.

1864   **MARCH 9**   President Lincoln names Ulysses S. Grant general-in-chief of all the armies of the United States.

MAY 4   Ulysses S. Grant opens a massive, coordinated campaign against Robert E. Lee's Confederate armies in Virginia.

MAY 5–6   The Battle of the Wilderness is fought in Virginia.

MAY 8–12   The Battle of Spotsylvania is fought in Virginia.

JUNE 1–3   The Battle of Cold Harbor is fought in Virginia.

JUNE 15   Union forces miss an opportunity to capture Petersburg, Virginia; this results in a nine-month Union siege of the city.

SEPTEMBER 2   Atlanta, Georgia, is captured by Union forces led by William Tecumseh Sherman.

OCTOBER 19   Union general Philip H. Sheridan wins a decisive victory over Confederate general Jubal Early in the Shenandoah Valley of Virginia.

NOVEMBER 8   Abraham Lincoln is reelected president, defeating Democratic challenger George B. McClellan.

NOVEMBER 15   General William T. Sherman begins his March to the Sea from Atlanta.

DECEMBER 15–16   Confederate general John Bell Hood is defeated at Nashville, Tennessee, by Union forces under George H. Thomas.

DECEMBER 21   General Sherman reaches Savannah, Georgia; he leaves behind a path of destruction 300 miles long and 60 miles wide from Atlanta to the sea.

1865   Southern states begin to pass Black Codes.

JANUARY 31   The U.S. Congress approves the Thirteenth Amendment to the United States Constitution.

FEBRUARY 3   A peace conference takes place as President Lincoln meets with Confederate Vice President Alexander Stephens at Hampton Roads, Virginia; the meeting ends in failure, and the war continues.

MARCH 4   Lincoln delivers his second inaugural address ("With Malice Toward None"). Congress establishes the Freedmen's Bureau.

MARCH 25   Robert E. Lee's Army of Northern Virginia begins its last offensive with an attack on the center of Ulysses S. Grant's forces at Petersburg, Virginia. Four hours later, Lee's attack is broken.

APRIL 2   Grant's forces begin a general advance and break through Lee's lines at Petersburg. Lee evacuates Petersburg. Richmond, Virginia, the Confederate capital, is evacuated.

APRIL 9   Robert E. Lee surrenders his Confederate Army to Ulysses S. Grant at the village of Appomattox Court House, Virginia.

APRIL 14   John Wilkes Booth shoots President Lincoln at Ford's Theatre in Washington, D.C.

APRIL 15   President Abraham Lincoln dies. Vice President Andrew Johnson assumes the presidency.

APRIL 18   Confederate general Joseph E. Johnston surrenders to Union general William T. Sherman in North Carolina.

APRIL 26   John Wilkes Booth is shot and killed in a tobacco barn in Virginia.

DECEMBER   The Thirteenth Amendment is ratified.

1866

Congress approves the Fourteenth Amendment to the Constitution.

Congress passes the Civil Rights Act.

The responsibilities and powers of the Freedmen's Bureau are expanded by Congress. The legislation is vetoed by President Johnson, but Congress overrides his veto.

The Ku Klux Klan is established in Tennessee.

1867   Congress passes the Military Reconstruction Act.

Congress passes the Tenure of Office Act.

1868   The impeachment trial of President Andrew Johnson ends in acquittal.

Ulysses S. Grant is elected president.

1869   Congress approves the Fifteenth Amendment to the Constitution.

1871   The Ku Klux Klan Act is passed by Congress.

1872   President Grant is reelected.

1875   A new Civil Rights Act is passed.

1877   Rutherford B. Hayes assumes the presidency.

The Reconstruction Era ends.

Charting a Course

In April 1865, with the surrender of Confederate general Robert E. Lee, the U.S. Civil War finally came to an end. Four years earlier, millions of Southerners had entered a war to protect their world, a world that included slavery. They were confident of their future and certain of their cause. But with the South's defeat, those who remained saw that future destroyed, their lands and their livelihoods in ruin. Plantations were burned out and abandoned. Weeds had overtaken the once fertile fields as former farmlands had gone to seed. Roads were pockmarked with the effects of artillery. Railroads that had crisscrossed the Southern interior had been destroyed, their tracks torn. Bridges had been wrecked, and locomotives had been overturned like turtles on their shells.

Across the South, guerrillas and Confederate deserters roamed the desolate and remote areas in search of plunder. With their husbands and fathers gone, many women were left helpless and had to defend themselves as best they could. Countless thousands—both whites left homeless by the war and blacks newly freed—scoured the countryside for a place to sleep and for food to eat. Plumes of smoke rose from homes, barns, and even whole towns set afire. The once proud Confederate capital, Richmond, Virginia, was a bombed-out shell.

The South's plan to secede had failed. The slaves had been freed. The Union had been preserved. Now, the next difficult task was ahead: How would the formerly rebellious states of the Confederacy be brought back into the fold of the United States? Should the South be further punished for its sins of rebellion and slaveholding? What must be the new life of the former slave? Could blacks and whites live side by side in a South without slavery? Who would decide the future of the South? How would the South be "reconstructed" in the aftermath of a highly destructive war? These questions were important ones, for in their answers lay the political, social, and economic future of the United States.

LINCOLN'S NEW PLANS

The rebuilding, or "Reconstruction," of the South following its defeat in the U.S. Civil War actually began before the war itself was over. By the spring of 1862, President Abraham Lincoln became convinced that one goal of the war must be to bring an end to slavery. That March, he proposed to Congress that the federal government give money to any of the Union's border states that adopted a resolution supporting the gradual abolition of slavery. This included the states of Missouri, Kentucky, Maryland, and Delaware. All Republicans supported this idea, and the proposal passed.

At first, none of the states took the bait offered by Lincoln and Congress. Lincoln's point, however, was clear: Slavery's future in the United States was shaky, at best. Congress made other proposals in 1862 that pointed to slavery's ultimate end, including the emancipation (freeing) of slaves in the District of Columbia in April, the banning of slavery in U.S. territories in

By the end of the Civil War, the South was reduced to smoldering ruins. Bombed out and burned down, much of the region either had been destroyed by Union troops or scorched by fleeing residents determined to leave nothing behind. Confronted with reuniting the nation, the federal government struggled through tumultuous political events and established new policies during a period known as Reconstruction.

June, and a new act in July that allowed federal forces to take the property of all Southerners in rebellion against the United States. This "property" included their slaves.

In July 1862, Lincoln became convinced of something the great black abolitionist Frederick Douglass had stated almost a year earlier. Douglass, according to historian James McPherson, had argued that "to fight against slaveholders, without fighting against slavery, is but a half-hearted business and paralyzes the hands engaged in it." On July 13, Lincoln began telling a few of his cabinet members that he intended to issue a proclamation about ending slavery, one which he had been working on for several days. Soon, he informed his entire group of advisers.

Lincoln's idea was to free some of the slaves depending on where they were living. The plan said that all slaves in states or parts of states still rebelling against the United States on January 1, 1863, would be declared "thenceforward, and forever free." The proclamation, therefore, did not apply to the "border states" where slavery existed, but where secession had not taken place officially.

With this proclamation, it was becoming more and more unlikely that slavery would continue to exist if the North won the war. But the future of slavery was only one factor that affected how the country would get back together after the conflict. There were other important factors to consider.

For example, before year's end, Lincoln issued another proclamation that began to set the stage for the future of the South after the war. Lincoln's "Proclamation of Amnesty and Reconstruction" was declared on December 8. The plan began to define the political landscape for the South. Lincoln used his constitutional authority to offer a pardon to all Confederates, as well as the return of any property that had been confiscated or lost due to the war, with the exception of lost slaves.

Lincoln also promised that those who had fought with the rebel states could be brought back into the Union as full citizens, simply by swearing an oath of allegiance to the U.S. government. The president's offer had its limitations. It did not apply to anyone who had served the Confederate government as a civil authority, a diplomatic official, a high army or navy officer, or as a major Southern leader, such as the Confederacy's president, Jefferson Davis. There was another part of Lincoln's plan: In each former rebel state, once 10 percent of the people who had voted in the 1860 election took the oath of allegiance, then these newly loyal "Americans" could form a new state government, without slavery. President Lincoln would immediately recognize each state and restore it to the Union, as if four years of war had never happened. Lincoln also expected the new leaders of any restored Southern state to provide for the state's former slave population. It was a simple, straightforward plan that was kind, understanding, and based on charity.

Lincoln thought long and hard in planning this proclamation. It was not based on revenge or on punishing Southerners to bring them back into the United States. It would not put Confederacy supporters on trial for treason, nor would it take away their property (with the exception of their former slaves). Also, only 1 out of every 10 Southern voters had to participate in the process. Lincoln had created the plan with the belief that the future of the United States would profit more from restoring millions of Americans back into the country, rather than punishing them for their political extremism.

When Lincoln created his "Ten Percent Plan," he did so from a position of strength. Even though the war was not yet over, the North appeared to have gained the upper hand. Beginning with the Union victory at Gettysburg and continuing through the last six months of the year, the federal strategy was starting to win. U.S. troops finally had gained control of nearly all of Tennessee, as well as significant portions of other Confederate states, including Arkansas, Louisiana, Mississippi, and Virginia. As Union forces gained military control of these regions of the Confederacy, the need for new, civilian governments increased. This led Lincoln to create his Reconstruction plan. The plan was intended to provide defeated Southerners with a short route to return back into the fold of the United States without further pain and suffering.

But even as Lincoln's Ten Percent Plan set the stage for accepting former Confederates, it also was creating divisions

During the Civil War, President Abraham Lincoln quietly drafted the Emancipation Proclamation, a declaration that would free slaves in rebel states. By shifting the focus of the war to the moral issue of slavery, Lincoln was able to garner international support and additional soldiers for the Union. It became the turning point in the Civil War. Above, Lincoln and his cabinet adopt the Emancipation Proclamation.

within Lincoln's own party, the Republicans. Lincoln's plan in particular drove a wedge between the president and Congress. Although many Republicans supported the Ten Percent Plan, some did not. The divide centered on three issues, all of which overlapped with one another. These issues were the emancipation of black slaves, the future status of those newly freed people, and the politics of Reconstruction.

THE WADE-DAVIS PLAN

There could be no doubt that some plan—whether Lincoln's or another—would need to be developed to set the course for freed slaves. Change was clearly taking place in the South. According to historian Eric Foner, by the summer of 1864, a white citizen of Chattanooga observed that life there was "so different from what it used to be" since federal troops had begun occupying the South. Although this was true for many Southerners, black and white, it was extremely true for the freed slaves. Teachers from the North were opening schools for black children, and hundreds of thousands of black men and women were working for wages, a new phenomenon for the vast majority of former slaves.

Even so, the new world of the black community after slavery had not been fully thought out. Northern abolitionists who had struggled to end slavery for years, such as Wendell Phillips, believed that freedom for slaves was not enough. They would

Lincoln and Slavery

No one is more associated with the end of slavery in the United States than Abraham Lincoln. Born in frontier Kentucky, Lincoln grew up on the prairies of Indiana and Illinois. According to historian James Oliver Horton, Lincoln's father had moved his family "partly on account of slavery." As a Baptist, Thomas Lincoln believed slavery was a sin, one equal to "profanity, intoxication, horse racing, and other human vices," Horton notes. At age 19, Lincoln saw slavery close up for the first time during a flatboat trip with a cousin down the Mississippi River. They traveled all the way to New Orleans, and it was there that young Abraham saw an equally young woman sold in the slave market. The sight sickened him. Later, as noted by historian Horton, Lincoln told his cousin: "By God, boys, if I ever get a chance to hit [slavery], I'll hit it and hit it hard."

While serving in the House of Representatives during the 1840s, Lincoln did speak out against slavery. In 1849, he introduced a bill to abolish slavery in Washington, D.C. The following decade, during a speech delivered in Peoria, Illinois, Lincoln referred to slavery as a violation of the principles of the Declaration

need education, access to their own land, and the power of the vote. During lectures in 1864, Phillips emphasized what blacks would need once they received their freedom. "The Negro has earned land, education, rights," Phillips said, as noted by historian James McPherson. "Before we leave him, we ought to leave him on his own soil, in his own house, with the ballot and the school-house within reach. Unless we have done it, the North has let the cunning of politics filch [steal] the fruits of war."

Many dreamed of a completely new world for Southern blacks, but some had their doubts. They only had to look to

of Independence. Despite all this, during the 1850s Lincoln was not prepared to deny slavery to Southerners where it already existed. At that point in his life, Lincoln was cautious not to be seen as an abolitionist. He simply wanted to be seen as a Republican who wanted to keep slavery limited to the South.

By the Civil War's second year, Lincoln turned to freeing slaves in some parts of the South. His Emancipation Proclamation, issued in the fall of 1862, declared all slaves held in rebellious Southern territory to be free. The proclamation had been carefully worded. He was fearful that he might lose the support of the few slave states that had not seceded from the Union—especially Missouri and Kentucky. Because of this, he did not take steps to free slaves there.

By the last full year of the war, however, Lincoln publicly favored the end of slavery. When he ran for a second term as president, he insisted that abolition of slavery be included in the Republican Party platform. When he was reelected, he took this as a sign that the nation favored an end to slavery altogether. When he spoke to Congress a month later, in December 1864, he supported the passage of the Thirteenth Amendment to end slavery, which had failed on an earlier attempt. When Congress passed the amendment in January, Lincoln signed it, even though his signature was not necessary on the proposed addition to the Constitution. It was his symbolic gesture in support of the end of slavery in the United States.

Louisiana in 1864 to wonder if anything had really changed yet. At that time, Union General Nathaniel Banks had been in control of the federal occupation of Louisiana, a Confederate state. Many in New Orleans, the state's largest city, had not supported secession. They began looking to the future and were ready to write a new state constitution without slavery, one that would give strong support to the freed slaves. But General Banks soon stepped in, favoring a more moderate Reconstruction plan. He called for new elections under the old pre–Civil War constitution and even changed a military order calling for the complete abolition of slavery in Louisiana. Even as Banks was working against radical Reconstruction in the state where he had significant power, Lincoln gave him his support.

Since Banks controlled the voter registration process in Louisiana, the moderates won the state election in February 1864. The state's radicals, who wanted to see a new constitution and more radical change, had lost. In the end, though, Lincoln encouraged Banks to push his moderate supporters to agree to a new, more liberal state constitution. Banks and the moderates agreed, and a new framework of state government was formed. This one prohibited slavery and established a public school system for blacks and whites alike. Still, even with the changes, the new constitution did not go far enough to satisfy the state's more radical people.

Congressmen and senators in Washington were watching events in faraway Louisiana. Some became concerned that Lincoln's Ten Percent Plan was too watery, considering that Lincoln had given at least some support to Banks's idea of moderate Reconstruction. Some politicians feared that Lincoln's plan did not require enough change by enough Southerners to bring about a different world of race in the South. Congress began taking bigger steps in support of a more radical Reconstruction. When Louisiana sent its newly elected representatives to Congress, they were excluded. During the 1864 election, Congress refused to recognize electoral ballots submitted by Arkansas,

After emancipation, people soon realized that former slaves would need more than freedom. Centuries of oppression and forced reliance on their owners had deprived slaves of the basic education and skills needed to establish an independent livelihood. Many Northerners moved to the South to become teachers or to create schools (above) to help ease the transition from slavery to freedom.

Louisiana, and Tennessee—all of which were states that had re-entered the Union under Lincoln's limited plan.

In addition, Congress began taking serious steps to create a Reconstruction plan of its own. It wanted to take some of the direction of Reconstruction out of the president's hands and put it into its own. Through the spring of 1864, multiple plans were under consideration. Historian Herman Belz recalls one congressman's critical view of it all: "Everybody abounds in schemes for settling the troubles in the rebel states and at least six plans a day are offered in the shape of a Bill." By July 1864, after months of debate, a bill was presented for a vote. It was the Wade-Davis Bill, named after its sponsors: Maryland Congressman Henry Winter Davis and Senator Benjamin Wade of Ohio.

TWO COMPETING PLANS

The Wade-Davis Bill was different from Lincoln's Ten Percent Plan in several important ways. First, Lincoln's plan only required that in each state, 1 of every 10 voters from the 1860 election take loyalty oaths. The Wade-Davis Bill required 50 percent. Also in the Wade-Davis Bill, those who took the oaths would not have the power to select state officials, as Lincoln's plan allowed. Instead, it charged the elections of delegates to a constitutional convention. Lincoln's plan allowed those taking the oath of allegiance to vote, while Wade-Davis only allowed people to vote if they took an "iron-clad oath," swearing they had never given support to the Confederacy. Wade-Davis also provided several legal protections in support of the freed slaves' newly gained liberty, and required the nation's courts to provide further support.

When the bill reached President Lincoln's desk, it was an immediate challenge to his own plan. There was pressure attached to the bill for the president, since nearly every Republican in Congress had supported it. Lincoln, however, was unwilling to approve the bill, since it would bind him to a more complicated, harsher approach to restoring the Union. In addition, Louisiana and Arkansas already had been accepted back into the nation under Lincoln's plan, and passage of the Wade-Davis Bill would destroy the progress made already with those two states.

In response to the measure, which needed his signature, Lincoln took a unique step granted him as president. He did not sign the bill. Instead, he used a constitutional option called a pocket veto, which allows a president to kill a bill by merely refusing to sign it. In effect, the bill sits on the president's desk until the end of the congressional session. Since it is left unsigned, the bill dies. Such was the fate of the Wade-Davis Bill. Lincoln did, however, state publicly that he would enforce the Wade-Davis Bill in any Southern state willing to adopt it. He said this knowing that it would be unlikely that any would, since the plan was more difficult to adhere to than his own.

Congressman Wade, Senator Davis, and many in Congress were not satisfied—nor were they going to accept Lincoln's decision. On August 5, the bill's two sponsors issued a harsh statement that became known as the Wade-Davis Manifesto. The statement gave a serious warning to Lincoln and was published in the *New York Tribune*: "Congress passed a bill; the President refused to approve it, and then by proclamation puts as much of it in force as he sees fit. . . . A more studied outrage on the legislative authority of the people has never been perpetrated." Further, Wade and Davis strongly suggested to Lincoln that, "if he wishes our support, he must confine himself to his Executive duties—to obey and to execute, not to make the laws—to suppress by arms armed rebellion, and leave political reorganization to Congress." Lincoln accepted the warning, but he still pursued his Reconstruction goals as he saw fit.

Lincoln's Reconstruction Legacy

O ther issues regarding Reconstruction and the end of slavery also occupied Congress in 1864. During the Civil War, the Republicans serving in Congress supported the emancipation of the slaves, the first significant step being Lincoln's Emancipation Proclamation. They also wanted the end of slavery to be part of Reconstruction after the war.

President Lincoln, however, was uncertain about this. He worried that if the slaves were freed during the war, their freedom would not last after the war was over. This was his fear, even figuring that the federal armies would win. Lincoln had the wartime power to take enemy property, which could include slaves. Still, such an action could be declared unconstitutional once peace, and the nation, was restored.

Of course, slaves had indeed been freed during the war. This happened through various acts, the Emancipation Proclamation, and even by military orders given by various Union generals as their armies occupied Southern territory. Nevertheless, an important question remained: Would the courts uphold the freeing of slaves through such means after the war ended?

EMANCIPATION OF THE SLAVES

With such questions in the air, the Republicans decided that the only safe and certain way to end slavery was through an amendment to the U.S. Constitution. The amendment would have to completely outlaw slavery.

The Thirteenth Amendment to the U.S. Constitution was passed by the Republican-controlled Congress in the spring of 1864. It was the first proposed amendment in more than 60 years. The amendment passed in the Senate by a vote of 38 to 6, which included two Democrats voting for the measure. Then, the amendment met stiff opposition in the House of Representatives. Larger numbers of Democrat representatives had been voted into office in the 1862 elections, allowing Democrat congressmen to defeat the proposed amendment 93 to 65. This left supporters 13 votes short of the two-thirds majority needed in order to pass the Thirteenth Amendment. For the moment, it was placed on hold.

With the 1864 elections, the Republicans gained new seats in the House of Representatives, and the call for the Thirteenth Amendment was renewed. The election, of course, also put President Lincoln in office for a second term. That meant he would continue to serve as the nation's chief executive while the process of emancipation and ending slavery continued.

Lincoln had spent election night in the telegraph room of the War Department in Washington, D.C. Around 2 A.M., it was finally clear to the president that he had, indeed, won. With that assurance, he left for the White House, where he found a party of reporters waiting to hear from him. Historians Donald Jacobs and Raymond Robinson retold the story in their book *America's Testing Time*. According to them, Lincoln said to the newspaper writers that he took "no pleasure . . . to triumph over anyone," and then added, "I give thanks to the Almighty for this evidence of the people's resolution to stand by free government and the rights of humanity."

By that time, the American people, both North and South, largely shared the president's stance on emancipation. Missouri and Maryland were both "border states," or states that allowed slavery but had not supported the Confederacy. In these two states, conventions were held in support of an amendment to abolish slavery as part of their state constitutions. In addition, three states within the Confederacy—Arkansas, Louisiana, and Tennessee—abolished slavery within their borders. Louisiana and Arkansas took this step as part of their adoption of Lincoln's Ten Percent Plan.

AN END IN SIGHT

One month after the election, Lincoln sent an important message about what he wanted from the newly seated 38th Congress. In the election, 55 percent of the popular vote had gone for Lincoln. He took this as a sign of approval from voters, a sign that he should see the war through and restore the Union. He also recognized that the first business at hand must focus on bringing back discussion of the Thirteenth Amendment.

This time, the pressure to pass the measure was intense. The Republican Party's national platform during the 1864 election had included abolition, and Lincoln was certain that the nation had spoken in favor of emancipation. In his address to Congress following the election, Lincoln's plans concerning emancipation were clear. Lincoln was insistent on the passage of the Thirteenth Amendment, and he did not intend to rely on Republican supporters only. So, he invited Democratic Party leaders in Congress to the White House to drum up their support for the proposed amendment. By the end of January 1865, Lincoln had convinced enough Democrats to join their counterparts in the Republican Party to vote for the amendment.

With his reelection and the victories of other Republicans in the House of Representatives, Lincoln was able to sign into law the Thirteenth Amendment and further the progress of Reconstruction. Above, President Lincoln delivers his second inauguration speech in front of the Capitol in 1865.

The amendment's passage through Congress was only a step, though. The proposal to change the Constitution then had to be sent to the states for their ratification, or acceptance. That process began almost immediately. Illinois voted for ratification on February 1, followed by Rhode Island and Michigan the next day, and Maryland, New York, and West Virginia on February 3.

Twenty states ratified the amendment by April, including three Confederate states—Virginia, Louisiana, and Tennessee. Additional states included Maine, Massachusetts, Vermont, Pennsylvania, Indiana, Ohio, Wisconsin, Missouri, Kansas, and Minnesota. Nevada, which had just joined the Union a few years earlier, also ratified the amendment. These states marked a solid beginning for the process of ratification, but seven states still were needed for it to pass.

RETURN OF THE RECONSTRUCTION QUESTION

The process of ratifying the Thirteenth Amendment continued across the nation during the late winter of 1865. At the same time, the issue of Reconstruction raised its head, bringing Lincoln and Congress back into conflict. In the face of an unraveling Confederacy, Congress again tried to flex its muscles and define how Southern states would be restored into the Union. Lincoln's Ten Percent Plan already had been applied in Arkansas and Louisiana, and a new government in Tennessee was based on the president's guidelines for readmission. Lincoln had hopes that his reelection the previous November would make Congress get on board and accept his plan. In his annual presidential message following the election, he had included a veiled message to Congress. As noted by historian Roy Basler, Lincoln said he would support "more rigorous measures than heretofore" concerning a reconstructed South.

Lincoln sat down with Republican leaders in the House of Representatives to work out an agreement. In the agreement, Congress would accept the reorganized governments of Louisiana and Arkansas. In exchange, Lincoln would support a plan similar to the Wade-Davis Bill that had been vetoed the previous summer. The new plan would be applied to the remaining Southern states when they were restored into the Union. It was a significant compromise offer by the president. The compromise also included allowing blacks to vote in the remaining

Southern states; however, moderates in Congress changed this to include only blacks who were literate and those who had fought as soldiers in the Union cause.

RADICALS TO THE FRONT

Then, Congress began debating with itself. Through January and February 1865, several votes were taken in the House of Representatives, each representing slightly different versions of Reconstruction plans. Radical Republicans voted down any proposal that did not give voting rights to all black men or any proposal that recognized the new government of Louisiana. Conservative Republicans voted against bills that allowed black voters. Democrats voted them all down. Since everyone was taking sides, no bill was passed. Meanwhile, in the Senate, radical Republicans, along with Democrats, refused to accept Louisiana back in the Union under Lincoln's Ten Percent Plan.

Compromise among the opposing sides in Congress seemed impossible. Although some congressmen and senators were disappointed, the radical Republicans were pleased. They were willing to wait until the war was over before working to convince the American people that voting rights for all black men must become the law of the land. In part, they believed the longer they postponed a Reconstruction plan, the greater the likelihood that Lincoln would come over to their side. Lincoln's changing positions on the war and Reconstruction over the previous four years suggested that the president had, indeed, gradually turned more conservative. Historian James McPherson explains:

> From 1861 to 1865, Lincoln had moved steadily to the left: from limited war to total war; from gradual, compensated emancipation to immediate, universal abolition; from opposition to the arming of blacks to enthusiastic support for it; from the idea of restoring the Union to the idea of reconstructing it; from the colonization of freed slaves to the enfranchisement of black soldiers and literate blacks.

Radical Republicans had set their strategy on postponing Reconstruction, expecting that President Lincoln would eventually come around to their way of thinking.

LINCOLN SPEAKS OUT

March 4, 1865, marked Lincoln's second inauguration as president. It was a rainy day in Washington. Despite the weather, the president delivered a short speech, one that recalled the circumstances facing the nation four years earlier at his first inauguration. He reminded the American people, both in the North and in the South, that a war had taken place, in part, over the

Lincoln's Assassination

April 14, 1865, is still remembered as one of the saddest days in U.S. history. The Civil War had just ended five days earlier. To celebrate, President Lincoln took First Lady Mary Todd Lincoln to Ford's Theatre, just a few blocks from the White House, to see a light British comedy play called *Our American Cousin*.

John Wilkes Booth was a well-known and popular stage actor who often worked at Ford's Theatre. A Southern sympathizer, he was upset that the war had ended with a Southern defeat. A speech given by Lincoln that called for voting rights for black male Americans particularly angered the bitter actor and spurred him to action. According to historian James Swanson, Booth resolved to kill the president as soon as possible, stating: "That is the last speech he will ever give."

On Friday, April 14, as Booth stopped by Ford's Theatre around noon to pick up his mail, he was informed that Lincoln and General Ulysses S. Grant would be attending a play together that very eve-

issue of slavery and its expansion into new territories and states. Now, Lincoln said, slavery was on the road to oblivion as the Thirteenth Amendment was on its way to ratification. Historians Jacobs and Robinson recalled Lincoln's suggestion that no Northerner or Southerner could have predicted "that the cause of the conflict might cease with or even before the conflict itself should cease."

These words were only building up to the famed phrases for which Lincoln's second inaugural speech was to be remembered. His words revealed the soft hand with which he hoped to restore his long divided nation:

ning. Early that evening, Booth met with his co-conspirators and laid out the plot that would target Lincoln, Grant, Secretary of State William H. Seward, and Vice President Andrew Johnson. Booth intended to kill the president himself, using a 44-caliber single shot Pennsylvania Derringer, and then stab Grant.

Booth arrived at the theater after the play had begun. Quietly, he entered the box where the Lincolns sat and took his place, unseen, behind the president. Since he knew the play, he waited until actor Harry Hawk spoke a funny line. Then, as the audience laughed loudly, Booth pulled the trigger, taking his place permanently on the stage of U.S. history.

In the aftermath of Lincoln's assassination, all the conspirators were either captured or, in Booth's case, tracked down and killed. Only Booth succeeded in his mission that night, and his success altered U.S. history. The years that followed the end of the Civil War likely took a different path than the one Abraham Lincoln had intended. Southerner Elizabeth Blair may have summed up the true loss of Lincoln to her fellow Southerners. Historian Doris Goodwin quotes Blair: "Those of southern born sympathies know now they have lost a friend willing and more powerful to protect and serve them than they can now ever hope to find again."

Hoping to derail plans for Reconstruction and return the South to its former glory, actor John Wilkes Booth assassinated Abraham Lincoln while the president was enjoying a play at Ford's Theatre with his wife and friends (above). Booth was on the run for 12 days before Union troops found and killed him.

With malice toward none, with charity for all, with firm-
ness in the right as God gives us to see the right, let us
strive on to finish the work we are in, to bind up the nation's wounds, to care for him who shall have borne the
battle and for his widow and his orphan, to do all which
may achieve and cherish a just and lasting peace among
ourselves and with all nations.

Supreme Court Chief Justice Salmon Chase, who had
previously served in Lincoln's cabinet, offered the president the
oath of office. No sooner had Lincoln spoken the words, the
weather shifted and the sun emerged from behind the clouds.
Chase recalled seeing the event as a great sign of better days
ahead for the Union.

The end of the war was near, though it was not yet over. In
Virginia, Lincoln visited Grant's army, which had laid siege to

Petersburg, south of Richmond, for eight months. Lee's forces had been bottled up in a stalemate of trench warfare. Lincoln had been on the scene as Lee abandoned his positions south of Richmond in an attempt to break out from Grant's relentless encirclement. Following the collapse and abandonment of Richmond, Lincoln had entered the Confederate capital and walked down the city's main street to the house that Confederate President Jefferson Davis had occupied as recently as two days earlier. There, he sat down in Davis's presidential chair, a symbolic gesture that the war was nearly over.

Less than six weeks following Lincoln's second inauguration, General Robert E. Lee had surrendered his army to General Grant at Appomattox Courthouse in southern Virginia, ending the bloody conflict. The two great generals signed the surrender documents on Palm Sunday, April 9. As Grant ordered the papers drawn up, he recalled Lincoln's words of "malice toward none, charity for all" and gave Lee and his men easy terms for the surrender.

When Lincoln received word of the surrender the next day, he was already back in Washington. The nation's capital was emotionally on fire. Many people took off work, and crowds filled the city's streets. Throngs went to local millinery shops and bought all the red, white, and blue bunting they could to festoon their houses, front porches, and picket fences. All over the city, regimental bands played patriotic tunes. That evening, dozens of bonfires lit the streets as fireworks blazoned across the night sky. Everywhere, people were celebrating, shouting, and cheering the hard-won victory. At no time during Lincoln's years in office had he or the American people greater cause to celebrate.

The euphoria of victory unfortunately did not have a long shelf life. By Tuesday, the president was out on the White House lawn, speaking to a large crowd of visitors about the practical realities of restoring the Confederate states and their citizens into the Union. There were critics of his plan who wanted more severe treatment of the South.

Lincoln stood firm, refusing to brand Confederacy supporters as traitors. He described the Southern states, according to historians Jacobs and Robinson, as being "out of their proper practical relation with the Union" and expressed his desire "to again get them into that proper practical relation." Before he finished his address, he signaled his intent to make a "new announcement to the people of the South." When he finished his speech and the crowd filtered away, neither the president nor his audience could have known that it would be his last address.

Three days later, President Lincoln was assassinated. With his passing, the future of restoring the nation and of readmitting the South would forever be changed.

New President, New Politics

A single assassin's bullet redirected the history of the United States. Through his death, President Lincoln had, symbolically, become the last casualty of the Civil War. Lincoln had served as commander in chief of all federal forces during the conflict, but he had been fighting his own wars with Congress, as well. He had called for a charitable approach to Reconstruction, one that did not punish the South. Instead, he had argued for a plan that would pave the way for reconciliation of the national landscape and the recovery of the national psyche.

Now he was dead, leaving Vice President Andrew Johnson as his successor. Johnson was a Democrat who would soon find himself caught up in the swirl of events that would set the course for his still-divided nation. Perhaps Johnson could not have inherited the presidency at a worse time.

ANDREW JOHNSON

Like Lincoln, Andrew Johnson was descended from the American frontier. Born to a poor family in 1808 in Raleigh, North

Carolina, Johnson was a tailor by trade. It was his wife who finally taught him reading and arithmetic.

Johnson took an active role in establishing the new Democratic Party in the town where he raised his family, Greeneville, Tennessee, in the late 1820s and early 1830s. He was elected to the town council in 1829. Two years later, he was elected mayor. His tailor shop became a gathering place for locals to discuss politics. Johnson was not outgoing or expressive like U.S. President Andrew Jackson, who was in office during this time. Still, Johnson listened to others, and his friends and neighbors saw him as a calm and thoughtful man known for "his manner, the level stare, that commanded respect," noted historian Gene Smith.

Although not formally educated, Johnson was a curious individual, interested in knowing why things were as they were and how people in positions of power could bring about

Ratification of the Thirteenth Amendment

Twenty states joined in support of ratification of the Thirteenth Amendment during the spring of 1865, just as Lincoln was beginning his second term. The next group of states would not be so easy to convince. Several states, including the "border" states of Kentucky and Delaware, failed to ratify the amendment, declaring it unconstitutional because ending slavery was a right of each state, not of the federal government. It would not be until December 1865, a year after the amendment had passed through Congress, that ratification was finally completed. Rounding out the 27 states necessary for ratification were Connecticut and New Hampshire, along with 5 additional Confederate states: Arkansas, South Carolina, Alabama, North Carolina, and Georgia. In

change. There was a small college 4 miles (6.5 kilometers) outside Greeneville where, on Friday nights, the students engaged in debates. Johnson began attending these debates, walking the distance to and from just to hear the various arguments. In time, he was even given permission to participate. He was a supporter of a strict interpretation of the U.S. Constitution, believed strongly in states' rights, and had little trust in the power of the federal government.

But even when Johnson was elected mayor, the wealthier citizens of the town looked down on him, since he was a common man who worked for a living as a tailor. Johnson was fully aware of this judgment against him. When, as mayor, he was not invited to a local banquet hosted by a Greeneville doctor, Johnson understood he had been insulted. He said to a lawyer friend, according to historian Eric L. McKitrick: "Someday I

all, the ratification of the Thirteenth Amendment, which ended the institution of slavery in the United States, had required the approval of 8 of the 11 former Confederate States of America.

More than 250 years earlier, Africans had been removed, usually by force, from their homelands and delivered to North America to become laborers against their wills. Slavery had existed by law in the British colonies for more than two centuries. The South—first as colonies, then as states—had never known a time when black slavery had not existed. Suddenly, an institution that had held down an entire race of human beings had been ended. No longer would blacks be considered another man's property. No longer could whites keep blacks from learning to read, from meeting in their churches, or from moving from place to place without permission. White masters could no longer sexually exploit black slave women. Freedom was now the word among African Americans across the South.

A man from humble beginnings, Andrew Johnson (above) was a Tennessee Democrat dedicated to fighting for the working-class people of his state. Although he was from the South, he famously broke party lines and refused to leave the U.S. Senate to join the Confederacy after Tennessee seceded from the Union. The Republicans and Abraham Lincoln rewarded Johnson's loyalty by appointing him vice president.

will show the stuckup aristocrats who is running the country. A cheap purse-proud set they are, not half as good as the man who earns his bread by the sweat of his brow."

JOHNSON IN WASHINGTON

Despite his humble means, Johnson was elected in 1835 to the lower house of the Tennessee State Legislature. He was reelected in 1839 and again in 1841. By the early 1840s, Johnson had the means to buy his first slave, a young woman named Dolly, for $500. He soon bought her half-brother, Sam. In his lifetime, Johnson appears to have purchased eight or nine slaves in all.

By 1843, he was elected to the U.S. House of Representatives and was off to Washington, D.C. Historian Gene Smith notes that Johnson was "the first tradesman or artisan ever sent to Congress from a slave state." In Congress, Johnson took his seat wearing a suit he had made himself.

As for his politics, Johnson regularly spoke out in favor of his Homesteading Bill, which would open up western lands and provide free land to anyone willing to move out onto the Great Plains and beyond. The Homestead Act would not be passed until 1862. As to other business in Congress, Johnson opposed government intrusion into the national economy by passing tariffs, and he generally voted against bills for "internal improvements," which included federal support for roads, bridge construction, canals, and even railroads. (He had done the same in the Tennessee legislature, and once opposed a bill for a railroad, claiming, "A railroad! Why, it would frighten horses," noted historian Gene Smith.)

Johnson remained in the House of Representatives until he lost his seat in 1852. His defeat was largely due to a scheme of gerrymandering, or redrawing the lines that divided voting districts in a way that favored a particular candidate. The gerrymandering scheme carried out by the opposition party, the Whigs, changed Johnson's district and lost him the election, but he came back in 1853. It was in that year that he just managed to win the governorship of Tennessee. He held that office for two terms, until he was elected to the U.S. Senate in 1857.

Once in the Senate, Johnson again campaigned for his Homesteading Bill, which was opposed by Southern Democrats just as their counterparts had opposed the bill in the House of Representatives. Johnson was known for sometimes going against his fellow Southerners by supporting issues they usually opposed. His support of the Homesteading Bill caused a rift between himself and the wealthy "planter class" from western Tennessee. It was the exact kind of "purse-proud set" that Johnson had struggled against all his life.

During the presidential election of 1860, Johnson came out in support of a fellow senator from Illinois, Democrat Stephen Douglas, in a race that pitted Douglas and Lincoln against each other. The Democratic Party split that year, and Johnson withdrew his support of the Northerner Douglas. He instead threw his support in with the Southern Democratic candidate, John Breckinridge. Still, the break between Johnson and his fellow Southerners was already too wide to mend.

Following the presidential election that year, which Abraham Lincoln won, talk of secession spread all across the South. South Carolina left the Union in December, and nearly every Southern politician began to throw his lot in with those calling for separation and confederacy. But not Andrew Johnson. When the Tennessee tailor sided with pro-Union Whigs against the secessionist Democrats in his home state, Johnson was considered a traitor to the Southern cause. As the Civil War unfolded in the spring of 1861 and Southern states were electing to fly out of the nest of the Union, Andrew Johnson remained loyal to his native country. After all others had left, he would be the only senator from a Confederate state who did not leave the U.S. Congress and join with his fellow Southerners in secession.

For a time, Johnson was a politician without a political party. As the Civil War raged, he aligned himself with the Republicans and the pro-war Democrats in the National Union Party. By 1862, General Ulysses Grant and other Union commanders had won enough battles and had taken control of enough of Tennessee to establish rule there. At this time, Lincoln appointed the loyal Andrew Johnson as the state's military governor. Then, in the 1864 election, Lincoln was in search of a new vice president. When the votes were tallied, a wide majority had reelected Lincoln, and Johnson would soon lay claim to a greater office than he had ever imagined for himself.

The Scope
of
Emancipation

Freedom was only the beginning of the new lives that blacks across the South would soon experience. There were, of course, difficult transitions brought on by the abolition of slavery. White owners suddenly were forced to give up the slaves upon whom they had become dependent for the work needed on their farms and plantations.

For some slaves, emancipation meant reunion with family members from whom they may have been long separated. Sometimes, with the help of their former masters, blacks were informed where they might find their loved ones who had been sold to other owners. Stories are widespread of slaves setting out over great distances in search of their family members. In one case, a Northern newspaper reporter encountered a former slave in North Carolina who said he had already walked 600 miles (965 km) in search of his wife and children who had been sold off four years earlier. Some reunions were sad, including separated spouses who discovered their marriage partners had married someone else.

A failed banker turned war hero, William Tecumseh Sherman led a force of Union soldiers through Georgia, South Carolina, and North Carolina in a military campaign known as Sherman's "March to the Sea." Sherman, an uncompromising adversary, vowed to "make Georgia howl," and attacked, destroyed, and burned almost everything in the vicinity of his army as they marched through the South (above).

One looming problem created by the end of slavery was the question of land. Slaves, by definition, had been property themselves and typically did not own any land. Many former slaves had worked in the fields of their masters all their lives and knew of no other kind of labor. How could blacks, emerging from slavery with no money, gain land for themselves? It would become a thorny issue. Just as slavery had not come to an end without the involvement of the federal government, so blacks began gaining property with the assistance of that same national government.

SPECIAL FIELD ORDERS, NO. 15

Union General William Tecumseh Sherman was one of the first federal officers to place land in the hands of black freedmen.

The general was engaged in his famous "March to the Sea" when Congress voted in favor of the Thirteenth Amendment. On January 16, 1865, just a few months before the end of the war, Sherman issued Special Field Orders, No. 15. This was a military directive that earmarked a strip of land 30 miles (48 km) wide extending from Charleston, South Carolina, to Jacksonville, Florida, a distance of nearly 250 miles (400 km). White families had abandoned most of this land, and Sherman chose to set it aside for black ownership. The head of every participating black family could receive 40 acres (16 hectares) through "possessory title." When the Union general provided the use of army mules

Southern Blacks Organize Against Black Codes

During Reconstruction, in response to questions from the Southern white community about how to handle the new freedmen, state governments began writing up "black codes," which were designed to limit the personal freedoms and economic and social opportunities for former slaves. These new laws kept blacks from buying alcohol, owning firearms, voting, or serving on juries. The black codes were so restrictive that some Southern blacks rose up against them and fought back.

Meeting in state conventions as early as 1865 and 1866, blacks protested the unjust codes in their state. Many who attended these conventions were ministers, teachers, and businessmen and had been free prior to the war. Few had ever been slaves. The conventions provided a forum where black delegates could call on whites and appeal to their humanity and their democratic principles, especially those found in the Declaration of Independence and the U.S. Constitution.

In Charleston, South Carolina, black delegates met at two different conventions. One was before the state's black codes had

to accompany the land grant, a new phrase was born: "Forty acres and a mule."

By the summer of 1865, 40,000 freedmen were at work on 400,000 acres (162,000 ha) of Atlantic coastal farmland from South Carolina to Georgia. Most chose not to plant and raise cotton, as many had as slaves, but relied on corn and sweet potato production. They usually worked in family units, steering clear of the gang labor they associated with slavery. In most cases, it was the men who worked the fields, intent on keeping their wives and daughters away from the fieldwork that many had experienced while held in bondage.

been enacted, and one was afterward. At the first convention, the blacks attending tried to make peace with the state's white leaders, expressing their "respect and affection" toward them, as noted by historian Hine. Delegates to the first convention even suggested that only literate men should be allowed to vote, whether they were black or white.

Once the state legislature passed black codes, however, black delegates called a second convention, where they called for the codes to be struck down. They also called for the vote, for the right to testify in a court of law, for access to public schools for their children, and for land to be distributed to former slaves through the Homestead Act that Congress had passed back in 1862.

Southern whites tended to simply ignore the calls issued by black state conventions, and they were certain they could keep blacks in secondary roles. Blacks were confused and angry over the many black codes across the South, and about President Johnson's Reconstruction policies that favored whites. According to historian Hine, one black federal veteran of the Civil War observed the opportunities still out of reach for most blacks across the South after the war, stating: "If you call this Freedom, what do you call Slavery?"

There were other situations and places where blacks gained access to land, as well. Some attempts to put land in the hands of former slaves failed. In 1864, the radical Republican congressman George W. Julian introduced a bill that extended the 1862 Homestead Act to include abandoned and confiscated Southern lands. Julian's proposal would have offered former slaves plots of land of 40 and 80 acres (16 to 32 ha). The proposal proved too much for many congressmen, and the bill was defeated. But Southern land still passed under black control. By 1865, about 20 percent of the farmland controlled by Union military forces was under the plow at the hands of former slaves.

One of the best examples actually took place on the plantations of Jefferson Davis, the president of the Confederacy, and his brother, Joseph, at Davis Bend, south of Vicksburg. As early as 1864, former black slaves, many who had been owned by the Davis brothers, leased thousands of acres from the military to grow cotton and other crops. Their 1865 cotton harvest yielded the black farmers nearly $160,000 in profits. These farmers formed a self-governing community, selecting their own law enforcement officials. Other former slaves across the South managed the same arrangement.

THE FREEDMEN'S BUREAU

Placing land in the hands of newly freed slaves was not the only answer to the question of how freed individuals might cope in a post-slavery world, especially if they remained in the South. To help address that question, Congress established the Bureau of Refugees, Freedmen, and Abandoned Lands, popularly referred to as the Freedmen's Bureau, in the spring of 1865. It was set up as a temporary agency to guide former slaves into the world of freedom, a world that could be quite hostile to them and their new status. The direction of the Freedmen's Bureau was placed in the hands of the army, and the "commander" of the program was General Oliver O. Howard. Howard, a strongly religious

Christian who had lost an arm during the Civil War, was more than willing to take the leadership of the bureau.

The bureau was designed as a giant umbrella of federal organizations whose tasks included helping provide land to former slaves, establishing education systems to teach freed slaves to read and write, helping negotiate work contracts between former slaves and white landowners, helping blacks through the South's lopsided legal system, and providing such street-level necessities as food, medicine, and transportation for blacks (as well as poor whites) whose lives had been dramatically altered by the war. Despite such lofty goals, the Freedmen's Bureau was always an underfunded program.

Throughout the years that the Freedmen's Bureau was active, fewer than 1,000 bureau agents were supposed to take care of the needs of former slaves across the entire South. The state of Mississippi, in 1866, only had a dozen agents. One of them was responsible for a county that included between 10,000 and 20,000 freedmen. Since the program was operated by the military, few agents were black, as almost no federal officers were black.

Despite strains in manpower and resources, however, the Freedmen's Bureau did what it could, establishing tent communities where homeless blacks could find shelter, food, and medical care. In all, the bureau issued 13 million rations of food by 1866, most including little more than some flour, cornmeal, and sugar. Doctors treated 500,000 former slaves, as well as poor whites, for diseases that ranged from cholera to smallpox to pneumonia. Still, for every one person treated, many more were not.

By the summer of 1865, the Freedmen's Bureau began looking seriously at land distribution to former slaves. Howard issued an order called Circular 13, which took Southern land that had been confiscated or abandoned, and divided it into 40-acre (16-ha) portions. However, the order was immediately overturned. By that time, the war had been over for several

months, and the federal government already was restoring land
back to former Confederates. Even Sherman's Special Field Orders, No. 15, had been cancelled and the land had been returned
to its original white owners.

This redirecting of federal policy was taking place through
the efforts of the new president, Andrew Johnson, who had become the nation's leader following the assassination of Abraham
Lincoln. Johnson had begun a program of forgiveness, one that
Lincoln himself might have approved of. That summer, Johnson
was intent on pardoning former Rebels, ultimately thousands of
them, and returning their land as a gesture of good faith. If they
were going to be given back their U.S. citizenship, after all, then
the federal government had to recognize their rights, including
property rights.

Suddenly, General Howard had to inform thousands of
blacks that the land they had been given would have to be surrendered and returned to their former owners. In one scene on
South Carolina's Edisto Island in October 1865, General Howard stood before 2,000 former slaves, telling them they would
have to give up their land. As historian Darlene Hine relates
the story, Howard appealed to the freedmen to "lay aside their
bitter feelings, and to become reconciled to their old masters."
A former slave answered: "Why, General Howard, why do you
take away our lands? You take them from us who are true, always true to the Government! You give them to our all-time
enemies. This is not right!"

Howard was moved to respond to the disappointment and
resentment expressed by former slaves who lost land only recently granted to them. When he went to Washington, D.C., to
plead their case, however, he was ignored. Both Congress and
President Johnson were intent, first and foremost, on restoring Southern states and their white populations back into the
Union. Confederates who had lost their land would now receive
it back again. To the former slaves, their freedom came with
significant restrictions and with limited meaning.

THE SCOURGE OF SHARECROPPING

Even during the months when land was given to former slaves, only a small fraction of them had received the use of any property. When the lands were returned to their original white owners, most freedmen had few choices regarding their futures. By 1866, the bureau even was forcing some former slaves to agree to sign work contracts with white landowners to provide, in many cases, the same type of labor they had performed when they had been slaves. Such contracts typically favored the white landowners, creating a legal contract between them and black workers. In some cases, the landowner did pay wages to his black laborers, but in most cases, freedmen were paid with a portion of the crop they produced. These contracts were usually good for a year, and the worker came into the arrangement with few rights. Sometimes, white landowners tried to get their black contracted workers to labor in gangs, just as they had as slaves.

This new labor system did not develop into the system known as "sharecropping" overnight, but the unfair, exploitative system was fully in place by the 1870s. As sharecroppers, the black workers were not paid wages and worked someone else's land in family units instead of gangs. Under a typical sharecropping arrangement, the white landowners provided everything the black worker needed to bring in a harvest: land, seed, farm tools, fertilizer, and work animals. In short, they provided everything except the labor. It was not uncommon for the black sharecroppers to receive one-third of a given crop as payment for their services. Yet it was almost as common for sharecroppers to be cheated out of their fair share of a harvest.

EDUCATING FORMER SLAVES

Although land was not part of the new freedom granted to slaves following the ratification of the Thirteenth Amendment, education was. As many freed people knew, the ability to read and write might well be their ticket to a productive future. Prior to the war, every state in the South, with the exception of Tennessee, had banned teaching slaves how to read and write. Some people defied such laws, and there were some schools for blacks prior to emancipation. Still, in 1860, 90 percent of the adult black population of the South was illiterate.

During the years immediately following the end of slavery, blacks of nearly every age pursued literacy. Freedmen were ecstatic when the Freedmen's Bureau made it clear to them that education was one of the bureau's goals. According to historian Eric Foner, one bureau agent recalled that when he informed a group of 3,000 former slaves that they "were to have the advantages of schools and education, their joy knew no bounds. They fairly jumped and shouted in gladness."

During the Civil War, action had been taken by a handful of people who predicted what the war's outcome would be, and some began teaching blacks to read. Northern missionary women went to the South during the war to open schools for slave children. Mary Peake, the daughter of a free black mother and an English father, led the way, establishing the first school for blacks in Hampton, Virginia. By 1863, in South Carolina, 1,700 black children were enrolled in 30 schools, where they studied under 45 teachers, both black and white.

Once the Civil War ended, a flood of teachers invaded the South, just as federal armies themselves had done. Several Christian organizations, including missionary societies, worked along with the Freedmen's Bureau to establish hundreds of schools for children and adults alike. As noted by historian William P. Vaughn, a Northern teacher working in Florida told of a 61-year-old black woman "just beginning to spell, seems as if she could not think of any thing but her book, says she spells her lesson all the evening, then she dreams about it, and wakes up thinking about it."

Black schools were held in all types of available buildings, from barns to stables, billiard rooms to warehouses, former

By working the fields and sharing the profits of the season's crops many former slaves believed that they would truly be independent and free. Sharecropping, however, became a system that allowed white landowners to frequently take advantage of the black laborers. Above, a group of sharecroppers gather around their cotton crop.

slave cabins to road inns and taverns. In the Southern cities of Savannah and New Orleans, schools were opened in the old slave market buildings. For many, their schooling was a hardship. Adults had to work their day jobs, which might include 10 hours of fieldwork, and then walk to the local black school to study reading, writing, and arithmetic in the evenings. In 1866, the Freedmen's Bureau alone spent $500,000 on education systems for freed slaves. Bureau officials often arranged the school sites and buildings, while the former slaves receiving their educations fed and housed the teachers. By the end of the 1860s, the Freedmen's Bureau was operating or had connections with 3,000 schools that were attended by 150,000 black students.

New education opportunities for the nation's freed people also included colleges. Northern religious organizations established colleges, universities, and academies by the dozens during the years following the war and into the 1870s. Most were teacher colleges, designed to train blacks to become instructors in elementary and secondary schools. The American Missionary Association, which primarily involved Congregationalists who had been abolitionists before the passage of the Thirteenth Amendment, worked together with the Freedmen's Bureau to open Berea College in Kentucky, Fisk College in Tennessee, Hampton in Virginia, Tougaloo in Alabama, and Avery in South Carolina. Again, in each case, these were teacher-training colleges at first.

As the path of education was laid out for the South's former slaves, many white Southerners were both perplexed and anxious. For those who believed blacks to be an inferior race, the idea of educating them always had seemed unreasonable, even absurd. According to historian Darlene Hine, one white Southern woman informed a teacher in a black school: "I do assure you, you might as well try to teach your horse or mule to read, as to teach these niggers. They can't learn." Some opponents of black schools became so desperate to stop them that they set schools on fire. In Donaldsonville, Louisiana, a female teacher at a bureau school was shot and killed.

Despite such extreme oppositions, most whites understood that blacks were perfectly capable of learning but had simply been denied such opportunities. Southern laws had seen to that. As Hine notes, one white opponent of black schools grudgingly gave in, stating: "Every little negro in the county is now going to school and the public pays for it. This is one hell of [a] fix but we can't help it, and the best policy is to conform as far as possible to circumstances."

Although black enrollment in Southern schools increased dramatically during the 1860s, such schools were almost exclusively black. Few white students attended. Most Southern whites would not attend or allow their children to attend schools that provided educations to black people. The federal government may have been in support of the establishment of education systems for freed people and their children, but it was not prepared to force schools to integrate. After all, even most Northern schools were not open to black students. In many areas of the South following the Civil War, there was no local black school, so blacks sometimes tried to attend white schools. In one instance, when black children attempted to attend a white school in Raleigh, North Carolina, they were not stopped, but the white children themselves refused to attend.

Johnson's Reconstruction

When Johnson first became president, he appeared ready to give harsh treatment to the states that had seceded from the Union. In addition, he made it seem that he wanted to serve as a friend and supporter of recently freed slaves. In 1864, even while still vice president, he had assured Southern blacks: "I will be your Moses, and lead you through the Red Sea of War and Bondage to the fairer future of Liberty and Peace."

Neither role—punisher of Southern secession and defender of the freedmen—ever became a successful part of Johnson's presidential legacy.

REDIRECTING RECONSTRUCTION

Johnson might have claimed to be a friend of blacks, but he was a Southerner who had owned slaves himself prior to the war. He also believed that blacks were inferior to whites. Even two years following the end of the war, Johnson still insisted that blacks should not be left to govern themselves. As noted by historian Hine, Johnson said that blacks had "less capacity for government than any other race of people. No independent government of any form has ever been successful in their hands. On the contrary, wherever they have been left to their own devices they have shown a constant tendency to relapse into barbarism."

President Johnson soon made it clear that he was not the tireless supporter of freedmen that he had claimed to be. Historian James McPherson notes how, after hearing a Union officer complaining that Lincoln had changed the purposes of the war through his Emancipation Proclamation, making the conflict a campaign to free black slaves, Johnson cried: "Damn the negroes! I am fighting these traitorous aristocrats, their masters."

It is true that from the beginning, Johnson had been opposed to the separation of the Southern states from the Union. As noted earlier, he had been the only senator from any of the states of the Confederacy who remained in support of the Union. But, although he spoke out enthusiastically about punishing rebels during the war, by May 1865, a month after the war's end, Johnson already was offering complete forgiveness. He gave out pardons to those who had rebelled against the United States, in exchange for their promise of allegiance to the U.S. government.

Under Johnson's plan that spring, the only rebels excluded from being pardoned were high-ranking Confederate officers and public officials, and those who owned property worth more than $20,000 (a significant amount of money at the time). Despite this restriction, such officials could make an individual application for a pardon, and many were accepted. By 1866, President Johnson had granted pardons to 7,000 important Confederate leaders and well-connected Southerners. He also had taken significant steps to obtain Southern land given to freedmen and give it back to the original white owners.

Johnson had wasted little time as president in taking significant steps in support of rebellious Southerners. To his critics, he appeared to be the friend of secessionists, former slave owners, and others who had led their neighbors into war with the U.S. government. Many whites who had been influential in Southern politics, economics, and civic life were once again in power, despite having given aid and comfort to the Confederacy.

Johnson, in fact, seemed to take nearly complete control of Reconstruction during the months following the end of the Civil War. He was the one who selected temporary governors in several former Confederate states. He was the one who set the guidelines for the leaders of Southern states as they called for statewide conventions to make arrangements for new elections and to regain their former membership among the states of the Union. As Johnson stood by, those same Southern state conventions provided no place at the political table for former slaves, nor did they guarantee black civil rights within those states. Johnson was the one who pushed former Confederate states to accept the Thirteenth Amendment, but he had no other agenda for them to provide anything but personal freedom for slaves.

THE BLACK CODES

Most Southern states of the former Confederacy began passing new laws that would set the boundaries for the freedmen who called that state home. These new state laws were often referred to as "black codes." At the heart of the black codes, Southerners were setting up a new social and economic system across the South.

In this new system, white landowners could rely on the freedmen to provide farm labor, just as they had during the decades of slavery. The rights of Southern blacks were restricted at every turn. Under the black codes, former slaves were required to sign labor contracts with whites. In some Southern states, such as South Carolina, any black person with plans to establish a business or other money-making venture in that state had to purchase a license, which might cost anywhere between $10 and $100. By these codes, black people under the age of 21 could be "apprenticed" to whites, with their duties included in the work agreement.

The black codes came so close to restoring the basic structures of slavery that employers could legally carry out corporal punishment against their black workers, just as they had been able to do to their slaves. Even the term "master" was used in the black codes to refer to this new category of white employers. Black workers were called "servants," not "slaves." Beyond the required work contracts for blacks under the black codes, the freedmen typically were denied their civil rights. They were barred from consuming alcohol, carrying a gun, loitering on public property, hunting, or fishing. Despite the new black codes, freedmen in the Southern states did gain some rights, including legally marrying, entering contracts, buying and selling private property, and testifying or suing in a court of law. They could not, however, vote—not until the ratification of the Fifteenth Amendment.

THE RADICAL REPUBLICAN RESPONSE

As President Johnson made his agenda clear to the American people, black and white alike, many Republicans initially gave the new president their support. There were those radicals, including abolitionists, who howled at Johnson's policy of easy forgiveness of rebellious Southerners and his weak program on behalf of the freedmen. Powerful Massachusetts Senator Charles Sumner—who had in 1852 received a beating on the Senate floor at the hands of a representative from South Carolina for speaking out against the South and slavery—thought Johnson's policies were nothing but "madness." As noted by historian Howard K. Beale, another influential Republican senator, Thaddeus Stevens, said in June 1865: "Is there no way to arrest the insane course of the President?"

Sumner, Stevens, and other Radical Republicans were angry that Johnson did not support the black vote. The end of slavery

Senator Charles Sumner (above), a Radical Republican from Massachu-setts, became famous after receiving a vicious beating from a Southern politician in reaction to Sumner's speech, "The Crime Against Kansas." Defiant and unafraid, Sumner also spoke out against President Andrew Johnson's Reconstruction policies.

automatically had allowed the Southern states to add a dozen more congressional seats, since the entire black population would then be counted for representation. The old agreement had been that slaves would only be counted on the basis of three-fifths for representation. In other words, a black individual did not count as one person, but rather as three-fifths of one person. Even after the end of the Civil War, freedmen did not yet have the vote, but more white Southerners were sitting in Congress.

Thaddeus Stevens:
A Man of Equality

During the years of Reconstruction, few members of the U.S. House of Representatives were more powerful or played a more significant role in the politics of restoring the Union than Pennsylvania Representative Thaddeus Stevens. His reputation as "The Great Commoner" not only addressed his role in helping freed blacks find their place in the post-war South, but it also referred to his support before the war of free public education in his home state.

As a member of the House of Representatives, Stevens's primary political goal was to speak out against slavery and on behalf of other minorities. Eventually, he spent most of his time campaigning for an end to slavery in the United States. By the 1850s, he was actively involved in the Underground Railroad, the secret system by which slaves were helped in escaping to the North.

Following the Civil War, Stevens became one of the leading voices among the radical Republicans, those members of the party who wanted Congress to take the lead in rebuilding the South and restoring the Union. He became key in the establishment of military districts within the former Confederate states to provide protection for the newly freed blacks. He also served to help along the orderly restructuring of Southern governments and the writing of new state constitutions without slavery in existence.

Because of President Johnson's resistance to some of the measures the radical Republicans took, Stevens pushed through the House a resolution calling for Johnson's impeachment. During Johnson's trial in the Senate, Stevens was extremely ill, yet he spoke out against the president. Stevens lived long enough to see Johnson acquitted.

Three months later, on August 11, 1868, Stevens died at age 76. In his honor, his coffin lay in state in the rotunda of the Capitol Building, flanked by a black Union Honor Guard from Massachusetts. His funeral, held in Lancaster, Pennsylvania, was attended by 20,000 mourners. Half of those who paid their respects were free black men. As to his final resting place, Stevens chose equality in death. He elected to be buried in the local Shreiner-Concord Cemetery, because it was the only one that would accept both blacks and whites.

Still, the majority of Republicans were not as concerned as Stevens and Sumner. Most thought that, in time, blacks would receive the vote and that they would be included more directly in Reconstruction. They were willing to give the president some time to "experiment," assuming he would eventually see more clearly the necessity of giving the vote to free black men. Nevertheless, radicals such as Stevens and Sumner would soon reveal they had no patience to wait for Johnson to see the light and change his course. They would set the agenda themselves.

RADICAL REPUBLICAN PROPOSALS

Within months of the end of the Civil War, Radical Republicans were campaigning for voting rights for freedmen. They believed that, for Southern blacks to be protected from political moves made by white Southerners, they would need the vote. More moderate Republicans were aghast at the idea of black suffrage. They preferred to encourage the spread of the Republican Party across the South and to cooperate with President Johnson's agenda.

Many Northerners, whether Republicans or Democrats, despised the idea of voting rights for blacks. Following the Civil War, bills calling for black suffrage were defeated in New York, Ohio, Kansas, and the Nebraska Territory. In the District of Columbia, a move to give the vote to blacks was crushed, 6,951 to 35. Some Northern states did take the lead in passing laws allowing blacks to vote, including five New England states and three states of the Midwest—Iowa, Minnesota, and Wisconsin. More Northerners were concerned with allowing former rebels back into the Union with minimal effort than they were with giving support to black suffrage.

At the end of the Civil War, Republicans outnumbered Democrats in Congress 3 to 1. Even so, Republicans sometimes failed to take advantage of their numbers because party members were split into groups of radicals, moderates, and conservatives. Those on the right, or conservative, side generally agreed with

The goal of the Freedmen's Bureau was to educate former slaves and help them mediate conflicts with white people in the awkward post-war transition. President Johnson believed the Freedmen's Bureau was too broad, and vetoed support for the new agency. Angry Republicans in Congress quickly voted to override the president's decision. Above, a racist poster denouncing the Freedmen's Bureau and voting rights for blacks.

the president, giving him support in his policies of simple forgiveness of the former Confederate states. Moderates felt that the president was not supporting enough significant change in the South regarding the freedmen, but they did not want to break with Johnson, fearing such a split would help the Democratic opposition. Radicals, of course, wanted bolder moves by Johnson concerning black suffrage and guarantees of black rights.

Despite their differences, however, the Republicans in Congress were willing to block the entrance of newly selected Southern representatives into their ranks. To do so, in December 1865, Republicans made arrangements with the House of Representatives clerk to fail to mention the names of Southern representatives as he called the opening roll of the new congressional session.

Congress continued to try and take the reins of leadership of Reconstruction from President Johnson. Again in December 1865, the same month that the Thirteenth Amendment was ratified, leaders in the House and Senate established the Joint Committee on Reconstruction, whose membership included nine representatives and six senators. The committee intended to lay down its own guidelines for allowing Southern states back into the Union.

The committee was soon investigating Southern abuse against freedmen. To fix the problem, congressmen took two significant steps: By late winter of 1866, Lyman Trumball, a moderate senator from Illinois, introduced a pair of bills designed to provide support for newly freed blacks. One was a money bill to provide more financial support for the Freedmen's Bureau, while extending congressional power to protect the rights of blacks across the South. The other bill was nothing less than the first true piece of civil rights legislation in U.S. history. The bill provided that any person born in the United States must be considered a citizen, which in turn entitled him or her to certain civil rights that must be protected by the federal government under the U.S. Constitution. The bottom line: Blacks and whites must be considered equal in their rights as citizens. The bill was a clear attack against the newly passed black codes.

Both of Senator Trumball's bills ran through Congress with few objections, and with support from nearly all Republican members. Unfortunately, President Johnson would not allow the bills to become reality, and he chose to veto them both. Johnson claimed that the one bill would establish an overly complicated federal system to run the Freedmen's Bureau, an arm of the government that could exercise vast powers over Southerners. As for the civil rights bill, he believed the legislation gave too much to blacks at the expense of Southern whites. As noted by historian Darlene Hine, Johnson observed: "In fact, the distinction of race and color is by the bill made to operate in favor of the colored and against the white race."

ANGER AT THE PRESIDENT

Republicans were shocked, disappointed, and angered by the Johnson vetoes. Johnson's negative votes caused a surprising move on the part of Republican moderates, many of whom were becoming more radical. It was then the president's turn to be shocked and angered. He had not expected Republicans to rally against him in support of the freedmen. He could not have been more wrong, as Republicans overrode both of Johnson's vetoes.

Johnson's veto of additional support and power for the Freedmen's Bureau not only solidified Republicans against him. It also drove him into further cooperation with congressional Democrats. After Johnson's veto on February 19, Democrats held mass meetings in celebration of the move. Three days afterward, Democrats came to the White House and sang in honor of Johnson. The president then spoke to them, delivering a curious speech in which he compared himself to Jesus being crucified and Radical Republicans to Jesus's betrayer, Judas Iscariot. The speech is noted in James McPherson's book *Ordeal by Fire*:

> If my blood is to be shed because I vindicate the Union and the preservation of this government in its original purity and character, let it be shed; let an altar to the Union be erected, and then, if it is necessary, take me and lay me upon it, and the blood that now warms and animates my existence shall be poured out as a fit libation to the Union.

To some, President Johnson appeared ready to sacrifice his political career for the sake of political reunification of the Confederate states. To others, he appeared to be drunk.

Republican Reconstruction

Republicans soon directed their resources toward protecting the legal rights of Southern freedmen. Much of their efforts went into passing the Fourteenth Amendment to the Constitution. The amendment was groundbreaking: If passed and ratified, it would bring fundamental changes to the Constitution by, in the words of historian Darlene Hine, "compelling states to accept their residents as citizens and to guarantee that their rights as citizens would be safeguarded." As the amendment was proposed in Congress, the right of citizenship was to be guaranteed to all persons born in the United States, which would naturally include nearly every black person. Such persons also would be made citizens of the state he or she called home.

REDEFINING BLACK RIGHTS

The proposal also specified the rights one has as a U.S. citizen and then offered to protect these rights, especially against the actions that might be taken by a state. As the amendment was worded:

All persons born or naturalized in the United States, and subject to the jurisdiction thereof, are citizens of the United States and of the State wherein they reside. No State shall make or enforce any law which shall abridge the privileges or immunities of citizens of the United States; nor shall any State deprive any person of life, liberty, or property, without due process of law; nor deny to any person within its jurisdiction the equal protection of the laws.

This amendment was a completely new definition of who blacks were in the United States and how the federal government must protect their rights. Just over a decade earlier, the U.S. Supreme Court had determined that blacks were inferior and had no rights that any white person had to take seriously. The newly proposed amendment raised the nation's black population to a status equal to that of whites. As the proposal was written, the federal government would have the power to deny representation in Congress to any state that tried to deny black citizens their rights.

The amendment sparked immediate controversy. Democrats in Congress were nearly all opposed to it. All the Southern states, with the exception of Tennessee, resolved they would not ratify the amendment. President Johnson spoke against it, even though he knew he had no real power to stop it, short of casting a veto to try and kill it. By mid-June 1866, however, the needed two-thirds majority of Congress approved the amendment. By June 22, Johnson informed Congress that he had instructed his secretary of state to send the amendment to the states for ratification.

Even then, the president blustered and protested, and he claimed that the American people should have been consulted on the matter. He went to Congress and spoke. As historian Hans Trefousse notes, the *New York Tribune* was less than supportive of the president's efforts: "Mr. Johnson rode his hobby into Congress yesterday. Nobody wanted him, nobody expected him, nobody felt he had any business there. His message was about as appropriate as though it had contained the bill of

JOHNSON AS KING SUPPORTED BY SEWARD AND WELLES. IN THE DISTANCE
HENRY WARD BEECHER, WENDELL PHILLIPS, CHARLES SUMNER, AND OTHER
ABOLITIONISTS ARE FORMED IN LINE FOR EXECUTION

*Locked in a losing battle with the Republicans, President Andrew
Johnson refused to pass the Reconstruction Act, a bill drafted by
members of Congress. Johnson, who was quickly losing allies, received
an embarrassing blow to his reputation when Congress passed a bill
limiting his presidential power. Above, a political cartoon depicts
President Johnson as king of the South in the midst of lining up famous
abolitionists for execution.*

fare for his breakfast, his latest tailor's account, or his opinions upon the cause of thunder." Johnson was beginning to be taken less seriously, even by Republicans. In July, this was made clear with Johnson's veto of a rewritten Freedmen's Bureau Bill. Congress overrode his veto before the end of the same day, with moderate Republicans voting against the president. In the end, the Fourteenth Amendment was ratified by July 1866.

A NATIONAL CAMPAIGN

Congress maintained its position of leadership of post-war Reconstruction. Johnson did not give up his fight, however, and continued to block congressional moves. Following the ratification of the Fourteenth Amendment in July, the president decided to take his cause directly to the American people. Even as friends and advisers told him not to do so, he headed across country, bound out of the capital for Chicago, St. Louis, New York, Pittsburgh, Cleveland, Indianapolis, and points in between. His "campaign" lasted for just over two weeks (August 28 to September 15) and was an absolute failure.

During speeches, he was forced to argue directly with members of his audience. He exchanged barbs and insults with hecklers. Through it all, he kept hammering away at the same mantra: The former Confederate states were loyal to the federal government and the Radical Republicans were the true traitors, those who blocked the readmission of the Southern states back into the Union.

Repeatedly, he spoke as a martyr, one willing to surrender his own life to restore the Union and uphold the U.S. Constitution. During a speech in Cleveland, according to historian Trefousse, everything went badly. Shouts from the audience not only interrupted the president, but they also made him look foolish, especially when he had compared himself to Jesus on the Cross. General Ulysses Grant had agreed to accompany Johnson on his tour, but he soon faked illness and refused to appear in the lecture halls with the president making a fool of himself.

Johnson emerged from his lecture tour humiliated. In the meantime, during the 1866 congressional elections that fall, it became clear that the president was hopelessly out of step—not only with Congress, but also with much of the American public. The November vote even surprised the Republicans themselves. They not only held on to their 3-to-1 majority in both houses, they also gained political seats in every Northern state, plus West Virginia, Missouri, and Johnson's home state, Tennessee.

It was clear to the Republicans that the November 1866 elections had delivered not only a clear victory to the party, but a sort of permission from the American people as well (even as they were uncertain exactly what that permission was for). Republicans focused immediately on the Fourteenth Amendment, certain the American people wanted to see its ratification.

Winning the election did not, however, automatically translate into a clear path to making the new amendment federal law. Ratification would require every state the Republicans had won to accept the amendment, plus a minimum of four former Confederate states that had not yet become fully "reconstructed." And President Johnson was not prepared to surrender leadership to Congress. He continued to fight the amendment, actively discouraging the legislatures of Virginia and Alabama from voting for ratification even as they were otherwise prepared to do so. One by one, he succeeded: Southern legislatures turned away from the Fourteenth Amendment, sometimes with every last state representative and senator voting against it.

A NEW RECONSTRUCTION ACT

For moderate Republicans, this was frustrating, even to the point of anger. As one moderate put it, according to historians LaWanda and John Cox: "They would not cooperate in rebuilding what they destroyed, [so] we must remove the rubbish and rebuild from the bottom. Whether they are willing or not, we must compel obedience to the Union, and demand protection for its humblest citizen."

Moderates reset their course to cooperate as best they could with Radical Republicans. During the three months that followed the congressional elections, they hammered out an important piece of legislation together. It was not easily formed. Democrats tried to derail the process, and the Republican Party's divisions engaged in long fights, a whirlwind of floor debates, and even congressional sessions that sometimes lasted through the night. Although Johnson protested against the new piece of legislation and vetoed it, Republicans passed the First Reconstruction Act of 1867 by overriding him on March 2, 1867.

The new act divided the former Confederate states into five military districts, each one under the leadership of a federal general. It would be the responsibility of the military to protect the peace, especially the safety of freedmen. They also had to protect private property rights, all while new, non-military governments were created. In every state, a new constitution would have to be written by newly elected delegates. The new constitutions would then be submitted to the voters for approval. Also, the Reconstruction Act stated that all adult males would be eligible to vote, with two exceptions: It would not include those who had actively supported the Confederate government, nor convicted felons. Every former rebel state that wanted to be readmitted into the Union would also first have to ratify the Fourteenth Amendment. Only then would the "reconstructed" state be allowed to send and seat its representatives and senators in the U.S. Congress. Radical Reconstruction had come to the forefront, defying President Johnson.

Congress's Reconstruction Act had placed the responsibilities and powers of the program into its own hands. Because

Union general Ulysses S. Grant (above) once had felt sympathy for Andrew Johnson, but the president's unpopular and sometimes embarrassing public statements caused Grant to distance himself from the Southern politician. Congress later passed a bill that required Grant to approve of every military order issued by Johnson.

of this, the president was furious. He already had described the measure in his veto message as, in the words of historian James McPherson, "a mad, infamous revolution." He spoke out with a vengeance, calling the new act, as noted by historian John Hope Franklin, "without precedent and without authority, in palpable conflict with the plainest provisions of the constitution, and utterly destructive to those great principles of liberty . . . for which our ancestors have shed so much blood." Johnson even claimed that the nation's blacks were not even asking for the right to vote. But there was little he could do, it seems. Vetoes by the president could be easily overridden.

A CHALLENGE TO THE PRESIDENT

Even as Congress seemed to have gained a significant upper hand at the president's expense through the passage of the Fourteenth Amendment and the First Reconstruction Act, they had other plans in the making as well. The same day (March 2) on which the congressmen overrode the president's veto, they passed another bill intended to target Johnson specifically. The importance of the Tenure of Office Act was that it restricted the president from dismissing his own cabinet members without Senate approval, since those officials had been placed in their positions with the "advice and consent" of the Senate. This was suddenly an issue, given the passage of the Reconstruction Act.

The Reconstruction Act intended to establish military rule over the former Confederate states in place of civilian, or non-military, government. The district generals held power that was technically being denied to the president. The generals were going to be able to hold military tribunals (military-run courts), suspend state law enforcement officials, and limit the authority of legitimate state officials. To Johnson and his supporters, including Secretary of the Navy Gideon Welles, this measure, as stated by historian John Hope Franklin, substituted "the decisions of soldiers for all the enactments and laws of eleven American states. It meant overthrowing Constitutional provisions about self-government with little concern." Johnson himself said the act subverted democratic principles. Congress refused to consider the president's protests. Even more than that, they passed an additional act that denied Johnson the power to give orders to any officers in the military, even though, as president, he was their commander in chief. All orders from the president's office to military personnel would first have to be filtered through and approved by General Ulysses S. Grant.

Johnson also was having trouble with members of his own cabinet. His Secretary of War Edwin Stanton was not only supporting Congress at the president's expense, he had even helped write up the act restricting Johnson's powers as commander in chief. Furthermore, Stanton had suggested to the radical Massachusetts congressman George Boutwell that Johnson might toss

Charles Sumner

Charles Sumner was a well-known lawyer, powerful orator, successful statesman, and a politician who would play one of the most important roles in the congressional program to reestablish the Union and bring the Confederacy back. Yet, his approach would make him one of the most controversial figures of his age. At one point in his political career, his opinions nearly resulted in his murder.

Sumner became a constant voice in opposition to the spread of slavery. When pro- and anti-slavery Westerners fought over the political future of the territory of Kansas, the Massachusetts senator delivered a speech that would have dire and personal consequences. On May 19 and 20, Sumner denounced the Kansas-Nebraska Act through his "Crime Against Kansas" speech, in which he was critical of Southern slaveholding. He was specifically critical of fellow senator Andrew Pickens Butler from South Carolina, one of the sponsors of the act that had opened up Kansas Territory to slavery.

These criticisms angered many, including Butler's nephew Preston Brooks, a member of the House of Representatives. On the afternoon of May 22, Brooks entered an almost empty Senate Chamber and attacked Sumner, beating him over the head with his thick cane, which was topped with a gold head. Brooks's viout his old cabinet and replace them with former Confederates, and then throw out Congress with the help of the military.

On March 23, Congress passed the Second Reconstruction Act, which added further details concerning the work the military commanders were to take in helping along Reconstruction. This included registering voters who had taken an "ironclad oath" of loyalty to the United States, as well as organizing state conventions and adopting new state constitutions.

cious assault continued until he cracked Sumner's skull. During the beating, an associate of Brooks's, Laurence M. Keitt, also from South Carolina, held a pistol on other senators who tried to rush to Sumner's aid.

Sumner survived the beating but took three years to recover from his wounds. He suffered from nightmares, powerful headaches, and head trauma, probably struggling with post-traumatic stress disorder. In the meantime, the Massachusetts General Court reelected him to the Senate in 1856, leaving his seat empty as a symbol of Sumner's and the state's resistance to slavery. Sumner returned to the Senate in 1859.

Even as the South divided from the North, Sumner was thinking ahead, working out a program for how the Southern states would be reunited with the North once the federal government won. He agreed with Lincoln that the end of slavery should be a goal of the war, but he went a step further by supporting citizenship and the vote for the country's freedmen.

Sumner campaigned on behalf of the Thirteenth and Fourteenth Amendments and fiercely opposed Lincoln's successors—Presidents Johnson and Grant. In 1872, Sumner introduced a civil rights bill in the Senate that would have granted blacks equal access to public places, but the bill ultimately failed.

Charles Sumner died in Washington, D.C., on March 11, 1874. His body lay in state in the rotunda of the U.S. Capitol Building and was buried in Mount Auburn Cemetery in Cambridge, Massachusetts.

One of President Andrew Johnson's biggest enemies in Congress was Thaddeus Stevens, a lawyer from Pennsylvania. A leader of the Radical Republicans, Stevens was a proponent of civil rights for blacks and strict military occupation in Southern territories during reconstruction. Above, a political cartoon showing the difficulties in the working relationship between Stevens and Johnson during Reconstruction.

SCALAWAGS AND CARPETBAGGERS

With the passage of this act, black leaders and pro-Union whites across the South (they would one day be known as "scalawags") began organizing a Republican Party in their former rebel states. Sometimes they did this alongside Northerners who were coming down to the South to have an impact on the political future of the region. These Northerners would be referred to as "carpetbaggers" after the suitcases they carried, which were sometimes made from carpet material.

The Reconstruction acts left the South numb. President Johnson was being ignored. The new acts seemed exactly what they were intended to be: harsh, forced punishments on the South. Uncertain where to turn, some Southerners suggested the courts. Perhaps the legal system would determine that the acts were unconstitutional. The temporary governor of Mississippi went to court with *Mississippi v. Johnson*, which was intended to keep the president from enforcing the Reconstruction acts. The Supreme Court refused to hear the case. In April 1867, Georgia's governor took a similar step, but again, the high court would not hear the case.

Johnson, meanwhile, continued to fight against these moves by Congress. He was actively advising Southern leaders on steps to take against certain congressional measures. On September 7, 1867, he granted official pardons to all Confederates. He hoped the 1867 elections the following November might bring him some additional support. But it was the Democrats who gained that year, with Ohio, Connecticut, New York, and Pennsylvania electing Democratic legislatures. Ohio, New Jersey, and Maryland also either voted to reject measures to allow black voting or to implement ones in favor of new laws clearly limiting the vote to whites only.

Such steps gave encouragement to President Johnson, and in December he spoke out against black voting rights. In a speech that month, as noted by historian John Hope Franklin, Johnson stated: "Of all the dangers which our nation has yet encountered, none are equal to those which must result from the success of the effort now making to Africanize the half of our country." With these words, Johnson was sending a message to Edwin Stanton and everyone else who was supporting black voting rights.

It was then that Congress stepped out to take on President Johnson as they had never challenged him before. They would attempt to remove his constant voice of opposition by removing him from office.

The Call
for
Impeachment

E ven as Congress had gained a strong upper hand over
President Andrew Johnson, he was still a significant opponent who could slow the progress of the House and
Senate in seeing to "real" Reconstruction. As military districts
were formed, Johnson always could send conservative generals
to run them. He could give narrow interpretation to the Reconstruction acts to put civilian power at its greatest level. He could
block and veto Congress at every turn, just as he already had
to an extent. In the minds of many congressional Republicans,
impeachment seemed the easiest way to get Johnson out of the
way. Once he was removed, they intended to replace him with
Vice President Benjamin Wade.

HIGH CRIMES AND MISDEMEANORS

It would be an extreme measure. Under the U.S. Constitution, the
House of Representatives was empowered to impeach the president, as well as any other federal official. The Senate was respon-

sible for trying and convicting him. Only a simple majority was needed in the House, but the Senate required a two-thirds majority. These steps were to be taken only when the charges were "Treason, Bribery, or other high Crimes and Misdemeanors," according to Article II, Section 4 of the Constitution. Only 5 times in more than 75 years had the House ever pursued impeachment charges, with the Senate only voting a conviction on two occasions. In both cases, the accused was a district judge. Impeachment powers had never been used against a standing president.

The idea of impeaching Andrew Johnson may have appealed to the Republican radicals in Congress, but it did not sit well at first with moderates. They argued that an official should be impeached only if the accusation also would bring about a conviction if the accused were a private citizen, not a government leader. The moderates did not like many of the steps Johnson had taken in recent years, but they did not think he had committed any outright crimes.

Radicals saw things differently. They argued that impeachment was not a criminal procedure, but that it was intended to punish an official for, in language quoted in the October 27, 1866, issue of the *New York Tribune*, "grave misuse of his powers, or any mischievous nonuse of them—for any conduct which harms the public or perils its welfare." Johnson certainly had been "mischievous" by their definitions, with his defiant attitude and disregard toward Congress, his multiple pardons of former Confederates, his embarrassing public speeches, his policies meant to block Reconstruction progress, and his public intoxication.

Action finally was taken on January 7, 1867, when a House resolution gave direction to the House Judiciary Committee to study the previous months of the president's conduct and determine whether he was, in the committee's opinion, guilty of "high crimes and misdemeanors." However, the radicals seem to have failed to look very far ahead in their scheme. Membership of the Judiciary Committee was made up mainly

of Republican moderates. Their report that June made it clear
that, unless Johnson was guilty of more than he had done already, impeachment would fail.

Nevertheless, Johnson could take only a small bit of comfort from the committee members. Back in February, one moderate had delivered an ultimatum to the president, as noted by
historian Michael Les Benedict:

> If [Johnson] fails to execute the laws, in their spirit as well
> as in their letter . . . if, holding the South in his hand, either
> by direct advice or personal example he shall encourage
> them to such resistance to progress as may tend to defeat
> the public will . . . the President may, after all, come to be
> regarded as an "obstacle" which must be "deposed."

These proved to be words that President Johnson could
not help but take seriously. He knew the radical element in Congress would continue to push for his impeachment if he stayed
his course of defiance. He soon seemed as though he planned
to cooperate with Congress and its version of Reconstruction.
He announced publicly his intention to do so. He would uphold
the laws passed by Congress. As Secretary of War Stanton and
General Grant selected generals to command the military districts across the former Confederacy, Johnson appointed them
like clockwork, knowing these commanders would not likely
do what he wanted, but rather, what Congress wanted.

As Johnson seemed to fall in line, so did many Southerners. This included important former Confederates, who believed
that Reconstruction, as laid out by Congress, was going to hap-
pen. Some thought that if they cooperated, they might get an
agreement from moderate congressmen to take the hard edge
off federal control. Southerners began courting blacks, encour-
aging them through political meetings and barbecues to join
with them and vote as "Southerners" rather than with the "car-
petbag" Northerners. But Republicans were able to counter such

moves and rally blacks to support their own party instead. With that, Southerners turned against Reconstruction, feeling they had little to gain. Once again, they placed their trust in President Johnson and hoped that he would somehow reverse the impact of Congress and push the radical Republicans out of power.

ANOTHER CHALLENGE TO CONGRESS

The president once again attempted to challenge Congress and its power. He still thought the Reconstruction acts were unconstitutional. Believing this, Johnson hoped to block their impact. When some of the military district generals appeared to use their power too heavily, the president spoke out critically.

He was especially critical of General Philip Sheridan, the Union's most important cavalry officer during the Civil War, who was in command of the Louisiana-Texas District. Sheridan had removed several elected state officials from their offices. Johnson asked his attorney general, Henry Stanbery, to determine whether Sheridan's actions were legal. Stanbery issued his opinion in June 1867, saying the Army's power over civil governments and their officials should be limited to police actions alone, and that Sheridan likely did not have the actual, constitutional power to remove elected civilian officials.

That summer, on July 19, Congress passed a third act of Reconstruction to fill the gaps in the previous acts that Stanbery's opinion had addressed. Congress passed this measure despite Johnson's veto. Some Southerners had figured out that, if they took the oath of allegiance, became registered voters, and then refused to go to the polls to vote on newly written state constitutions, they could defeat the measure because not enough registered voters had voted in its favor. Then, in March 1868, a fourth Reconstruction measure changed the approval process of a proposed state constitution by only requiring that a majority of the votes actually cast supported the constitution, even if many registered voters did not vote at all.

Desperate to restrict Congress's power, President Andrew Johnson excluded no one in his attempts to reestablish his authority, not even Civil War hero General Philip Sheridan. Johnson hoped to nullify the Reconstruction acts created by Congress by using Sheridan as a scapegoat. Above, General Philip Sheridan rides into battle during the Civil War.

In the meantime, impeachment questions had come up again. Johnson had demonstrated to the Radical Republicans that he was not genuine in his intent to support the laws Congress passed to monitor Southern progress. Moderates still were leery of impeachment, however, fearing the move would turn Johnson into a martyred president. They were not happy with Johnson, of course, and one moderate congressman, according to historian Michael Les Benedict, noted that "the President . . . does continue to do the most provoking things. If he isn't impeached it won't be his fault."

Then, Johnson made a decision that riled even the moderates. He had stewed as Secretary of War Edwin Stanton had continually supported Congress's agenda for Reconstruction. In August 1867, as the Senate adjourned, Johnson took the step he had long considered: He suspended Stanton. The Tenure of Office Act clearly had limited the president from such a move, but Johnson did it anyway, knowing he would not have to deal with the Senate for several months.

In the meantime, he appointed Ulysses Grant as the temporary secretary of war. Grant only accepted the role to, as noted by historian James McPherson, "serve as a buffer between the President and the army, in order to prevent Johnson from doing more mischief." Johnson also replaced military district generals Philip Sheridan and Daniel Sickles, even as Grant wrote a letter to the president and tried to talk him out of the moves.

When the Senate returned to session and began to bluster about Johnson's moves, Grant chose to turn the War Department back to Edwin Stanton. He did this on January 14, 1868, not wanting to be charged with defying the Tenure of Office Act. Angry letters sent between the general and the president made the front pages of U.S. newspapers.

Johnson, however, would not cower. On February 21, he ordered Stanton to surrender his position as secretary of the War Department. Senate radicals convinced Stanton that he should stand fast and defy the president. The following day,

Johnson's new appointee, Adjutant General Lorenzo Thomas, showed up at Stanton's office at the War Department. When Thomas got to the office, he found that Stanton had barricaded himself in and would not surrender his office keys.

A VOTE TO IMPEACH

Johnson's move was a clear challenge to congressional authority and to the Tenure of Office Act. Even moderates began to clamor for impeachment. On February 24, just three days following the president's refiring of Stanton, the House voted to impeach Andrew Johnson. The vote closely followed party lines, 126 to 47. Perhaps ironically, the overheated congressmen impeached the president even before they bothered to write up a list of charges or articles of impeachment. Only afterward did they select a team of congressional prosecutors, including Thaddeus Stevens, George Julian, Benjamin Butler, John Logan, and George Boutwell. They then drew up a list of charges that included 11 counts against Johnson covering a wide variety of offenses that equaled "high crimes and misdemeanors."

The first eight charges were connected to the firing of Secretary Stanton and Johnson's intent to replace him with a secretary of his choosing, without the consent of the Senate. The ninth charge accused the president of trying to convince the military commander in Washington, D.C., to violate the Command of the Army Act by responding directly to him. The tenth charge was written by Benjamin Butler, a less-than-accomplished Union general during the Civil War. This charge was a bit vague, accusing Johnson of, as noted by historian James McPherson, trying to "excite the odium and resentment of all the good people of the United States against Congress and the laws by it duly and constitutionally enacted." The last of the charges was merely a collection of all the previous charges.

For many, these steps went upon ground that had never before been covered. The details of Johnson's trial would have

160   HARPER'S WEEKLY.

WAR OFFICE

THE SITUATION.

When Johnson removed Secretary of War Edwin Stanton, Radical Republicans in Congress and the Senate moved to impeach the president. Above, a political cartoon of Ulysses S. Grant and Edwin Stanton about to fire a cannon labeled "Congress" with a rammer called "Tenure of Office" at President Johnson and his newly appointed secretary of war, Lorenzo Thomas.

to be worked out as best anyone could determine. Although the Constitution granted power to the Senate to try impeachment cases, it also called on the chief justice of the Supreme Court to serve as the presiding judge. The trial itself began on March 4 and dragged on for 11 long weeks.

To Johnson's advantage, he had a strong team of legal minds, some of the most important attorneys in the country. He paid all five of them $2,000 each, out of his own pocket. Henry Stanbery, Johnson's attorney general, was one of the five, but first he had resigned from his cabinet post to avoid any accusation of conflict of interest.

Also included was William M. Evarts, who would serve one day as secretary of state, as well as attorney general. Soon, he would be supporting General Grant for the presidency. Johnson's selection of Evarts was curious. Just four months earlier, Evarts, one of the most well-known lawyers in the country, had spoken out against Johnson under a large banner that read: ANDREW JOHNSON: TRAITOR, RENEGADE, OUTCAST. Once he had agreed to defend the president, however, he put his personal dislike of Johnson aside.

Another of Johnson's defenders was Benjamin R. Curtis, a former Supreme Court justice from Boston, who had written against the majority of the court in the *Dred Scott* case, an all-important race case dating back more than a decade. His conservative Republican principles made him a solid member of the team. The third member of the team, Ohio Democrat William S. Groesbeck, was described by historian Trefousse as "a slender figure with a massive head, a hooked nose, and a projecting chin, which gave him the look of a Cicero." Groesbeck was a well-respected attorney who had made friends with the president during the Civil War. Another friend and member of Johnson's legal counsel was Thomas A.R. Nelson, whom the president picked personally since he was a fellow Tennessean he could trust.

TRYING THE PRESIDENT'S CASE

During the trial, Johnson's defense team appeared to have greater legal skill than those chosen to prosecute the president and his case. In a broad sense, Johnson's defense centered on three basic legal arguments:

- Impeachment should never take place against a government official unless his guilt lies in having committed some criminal offense that would normally land him in a criminal court as a private citizen.
- President Johnson had committed no such crime by his actions, which had been designed to bring about a test of the constitutionality of the Tenure of Office Act.

- The Tenure of Office Act had been written to apply to cabinet officers "during the term of the president by whom they may have been appointed." Because of this, no case could be made against Johnson's removal of Edwin Stanton, since Stanton had been appointed by President Lincoln, not Johnson.

This final argument was significant, since 9 of the 11 charges had to do with either the removal of Stanton or Johnson's supposed misdeeds involving General Lorenzo Thomas. (The other two focused on Johnson's alleged defiant attitude toward the authority of Congress and his "pattern" of disgracing the legislative branch.) Even more important, perhaps, was the fact that the official reasons for the charges against Johnson did not include the specific reasons why the Republicans wanted to pursue impeachment. These reasons included his political philosophy, his lackluster methods of enforcing the Reconstruction acts, and, especially, his absolute inability to lead as president.

Johnson's advisers agreed early on that the president must not ever appear to take the trial proceedings seriously. To avoid this, he must never actually attend the proceedings in person. Johnson protested this view, as he wanted to answer his opponents and put the entire process to rest. Certainly, the trial prosecutors wanted the president to be there. As noted by historian Gene Smith, Benjamin Butler in particular "pictured the Great Criminal literally standing before the bar of justice, forbidden to take a seat until it should be the Senate's pleasure that he do so." When it became clear that his colleagues would not force the presence of Johnson at the trial, Butler was greatly disappointed, Smith noted. Butler felt that his colleagues were "too weak in the knees or back."

Unfortunately for those who wanted to see Johnson convicted, Butler handled much of the prosecution of the trial against the president. Butler and his associates took the leadership and sometimes carried themselves with less politeness than the occasion called for. They would sometimes liven up trial

Salmon P. Chase

During his long career of public service, Salmon P. Chase wore a variety of hats, serving variously as a governor, senator, secretary of the treasury, and the sixth Supreme Court chief justice. But the role he played during the impeachment trial of President Johnson would become the one for which he would be most often remembered.

In 1849, Chase won a U.S. Senate seat as a Free Soil Party candidate from Ohio. During his time in the Senate, Chase spoke out against slavery and its Western expansion. He spoke out against the Compromise of 1850 that opened up the American Southwest to slavery, as well as the Kansas-Nebraska Act of 1854, which allowed citizens to vote to decide whether slavery would be accepted in those two Northern territories. That same year, Chase was key in forming a new political party to replace the dying Whigs: the Republican Party. He soon would serve as Ohio's first Republican governor, giving his support to women's rights, free public education, and prison reform.

He served as secretary of the Treasury Department in President Lincoln's cabinet, a position that required him to design the first U.S. federal currency. In 1864, Lincoln appointed Chase to the U.S. Supreme Court, where Chase served as a justice until his death in 1873. While chief justice, he appointed the first African-American attorney, John Rock, to argue cases before the U.S. Supreme Court. It was during his tenure on the bench that Chase presided at the impeachment trial of President Johnson.

During Johnson's trial, Chief Justice Chase constantly steered the legal proceedings into a narrow channel of legal issues, forcing the prosecution team to focus almost exclusively on the president's removal of Stanton as secretary of the War Department. By doing so, Chase nearly restrained the House managers from hammering away with any effect on the president's general policies or his alleged "crimes."

That same year, Chase tried to gain the Democratic Party's nomination for president, but he failed because of his support of voting rights for black men. He died in New York City in 1873.

sessions by eating large slices of cheese that they cut off a roll with their penknives. Thaddeus Stevens, under different circumstances, likely would have served as the dominant one among the "managers" assigned to try Johnson. However, Stevens was not healthy, and he even appeared close to dying. He was selected as the chair of the managers but had to take a less active role than he might have liked. As described by historian Smith, Stevens was "thin and pale, his eyes swallowed up in cavernous sockets, his skull showing through the skin, he sat swathed in blankets during the meetings of the board of managers."

THE TRIAL BEGINS

The event began on the afternoon of March 4, with the Senate's doors opening and the committee of managers entering the chamber in pairs, locked arm in arm. Vice President Benjamin Wade was in his seat as president pro tem of the Senate. As the managers seated themselves, the 11 charges against President Johnson were read. It all took 20 minutes to present completely and was finished, as noted by historian Smith, with the reader stating that the counts were presented by the House and in the names "of all the people of the United States, against Andrew Johnson, President of the United States, in maintenance and support of their impeachment against him for high crimes and misdemeanors in office." Wade then stated that the Senate would take the responsibility of hearing the case.

On the following day, March 5, the Senate galleries were full of spectators. Vice President Wade no longer presided. He was replaced by Chief Justice Salmon Chase, as prescribed by the Constitution in such cases. For all practical purposes, the Senate was serving as jury. Chase swore them in, with words recalled by historian Smith: "I do solemnly swear that in all things pertaining to the trial of the impeachment of Andrew Johnson, President of the United States, I will do impartial justice, according to the Constitution and the laws: So help me God."

Andrew Johnson was the first president ever to face impeachment proceedings (above). Although the Radical Republicans in the Senate and House of Representatives had accused Johnson of violating the Tenure of Office Act, it was clear that differing opinions regarding Reconstruction had caused a rift between Congress and the president.

Following the swearing in, questions were discussed regarding Benjamin Wade's place in the proceedings. After all, if the president was removed from office, Wade would become president. The senators decided to allow Wade to hear the case as one of their number, despite his conflict of interest.

Then, the court was adjourned until March 15 to give time for both sides to establish their strategies. During those days,

Johnson was informed that Wade was already choosing men to serve in his cabinet. Overall, the president remained calm during these otherwise tense days. He said that it was in God's hands. When stories circulated that Johnson had become superstitious in his beliefs, he was buried in messages from spiritualists, some even claiming to have received messages from Lincoln about what Johnson should do to defend himself.

The Senate Trial

O n March 13, the Senate gathered together again to proceed with the trial. Chief Justice Salmon Chase, wearing his Supreme Court robes, opened the session, calling for the president to appear to meet the charges. Historian Gene Smith recalls Chase's words: "Andrew Johnson, President of the United States, appear and answer to the articles of impeachment exhibited against you by the House of Representatives of the United States." Although everyone present knew the president would not be attending the sessions, the majority still turned toward the main entrance of the chamber. The doors opened as Benjamin Butler entered. Anxious laughter filled the room while a perplexed Butler could only wonder what he had missed.

LEGAL PROCEEDINGS

With the session officially begun, former Attorney General Stanbery rose to say that his team was not fully prepared and it needed more time to go over the case. Stanbery suggested 40 days. Butler answered in outrage, stating that God had destroyed the whole world in a flood in that amount of time (referring to the Biblical story of Noah and the great flood). Stanbery was granted a 10-day delay.

During the days until the trial would begin again, senators regularly received letters and telegrams demanding the successful prosecution of the president. Many politicians began to feel that Johnson's trial verdict was already decided. Sumner and Butler certainly thought so. General Grant, who would soon become the Republican nominee for president, was ready to be rid of Johnson. Grant was furious that his reputation had been damaged from his time as temporary secretary of war. Thaddeus Stevens, on the other hand, was less certain of the outcome. Convicting Johnson would require a two-thirds majority vote in favor in the Senate, which translates into 36 out of 54 senators. The House had only needed a simple majority to impeach the president. The difference between a majority and 2 out of every 3 members of the Senate was a significant difference.

On March 23, Johnson's defense team visited the White House before making its way to the Senate. Johnson had recently suggested that he wanted to attend the trial, but as his defense team left the White House, the president said nothing of it and sent them out the door. Standing on the White House portico, according to historian Smith, Johnson said: "Gentlemen, my case is in your hands. I feel sure that you will protect my interests." In fact, Johnson's seeming calm with his defense team did not mirror his true exasperations about the events that were spinning out of his control. Historian Hans Trefousse notes that the president could not have been more frustrated. Trefousse recalled Johnson's words: "They have impeached me for a violation of the Constitution and the laws. Have I not been struggling, ever since I occupied this chair, to uphold the Constitution which they are trampling under foot?"

As the trial opened again, the Senate gallery was packed with visitors. To attend, one had to have a special yellow entrance ticket. Each senator had four to hand out and each representative was given two. The session opened at 1 P.M. with Evarts taking the floor. The president's counsel began by stating that the Tenure of Office Act, so crucial in establishing Johnson's guilt or innocence, was unconstitutional. With it, Congress had stolen the power granted to the president under the Constitution. As to accusations connected to Johnson defaming Congress during his cross-country speaking tour, it was the president's right of free speech that was being questioned, a right the Constitution granted him. Following Evarts's presentation, the Senate adjourned.

The following day, the trial reopened, again at 1 P.M. Benjamin Butler took the floor wearing a black evening suit and white tie. Butler began in dramatic fashion, stating that the country was, for the first time, trying its highest official. His voice rose to emphasize his words. As noted by historian Smith, Butler stated of Johnson that, "by murder most foul he succeeded to the Presidency, and is the elect of an assassin to that high office!" Johnson had challenged Congress, Butler said. He had overridden the Tenure of Office Act. His behavior was criminal and tyrannical.

As Butler spoke of Johnson's national speaking tour, he mocked the president for shouting down from his hotel window one night to a crowd of street thugs, telling them of the evil motives of the U.S. Congress. His shouts had only drawn jeers, cat calls, and hisses from "a noisy crowd of men and boys, washed and unwashed, drunk and sober, black and white," according to historian Smith. Butler continued with high drama for three solid hours, until he finally finished, as Smith notes, with a deathless phrase: "I speak, therefore, not the language of exaggeration, but the words of truth and soberness, that the future political welfare and liberties of all men hang trembling on the decision of the hour."

Refusing to attend his own impeachment hearing, Andrew Johnson relied on his legal defense team to argue his case. Although the public and the Senate were eager to confront the president about his supposed violations of the U.S. Constitution and the Tenure of Office Act, Johnson was unwilling to be a part of the proceedings. Above, an admittance ticket for Johnson's impeachment hearing.

WEEKS OF TRIAL

With each day of the trial, positive public opinion seemed to shy more and more from Johnson. The newspapers were calling for his conviction. The famous editor of the *New York Tribune*, Horace Greeley, called for Johnson's removal. Greeley claimed more than he could have known about the president, saying Johnson not only had violated the Tenure of Office Act, but that he was also guilty of treason, public drunkenness, adultery, even murder. In the meantime, members of Johnson's cabinet tried to console and encourage him. As early as March 16, Stanbery told the president he was sure of victory, that he could even feel it in his bones. Secretary of State Seward even bet a basket of champagne that Johnson would weather the trial successfully.

During the days that followed, it seemed that many senators had decided a verdict. Testimony continued, witnesses were called, and documents—Johnson's order to discharge Stanton, for example—were entered as evidence. Most of the facts of the case, however, already were well known. The testimony only confirmed the opinions of the various senators, as many of their minds already were made up. The trial began to border on repetition and tedium.

During these weeks of trial, the president went about his normal duties and routines, trying to project his calm in the face of extreme political challenge. He hosted dinner parties at the White House, with his daughters, Mary and Martha, serving as hostesses. He continued his public appearances, making private visits and attending weddings and funerals, including that of his steward, William Slade, who died of edema in mid-March. Johnson went to Slade's funeral on April 18. On April 22, late in the trial, he attended a socially important Washington wedding. He went to church, a local Presbyterian congregation on New York Avenue. One Sunday, he attended a Catholic church and listened to a sermon about a pair of Roman brothers, Tiberius and Gaius Gracchus. The brothers were senators who tried to put in place reforms on behalf of the Roman poor, only to be killed through Senate conspiracy. According to historian Hans Trefousse, Johnson was led to later comment: "This American Senate is as corrupt as the Roman Senate." Throughout the entire trial, President Johnson believed he was being subjected to an extreme injustice motivated by little more than politics.

THE DEFENSE TAKES ITS TURN

The prosecution, the trial managers, had taken three weeks to present its case against the president. On April 9, the defense began to make its case. Benjamin Curtis took the reins and delivered a brilliant speech, making the point that Lincoln, not Johnson, had appointed Stanton. Therefore, Johnson must not be considered included under the Tenure of Office Act. Besides, Stanton was still the secretary of war. Johnson had only made an *attempt* to remove him. Any questions about Stanton being discharged were purely theoretical.

Beyond that point, Curtis said, the president certainly had the authority to challenge a law passed by Congress, especially if he thought it violated the Constitution. Also, regarding Johnson's expressions of his strong opinions regarding Congress and its actions, he had only been exercising his right of free speech.

Then the defense team began calling witnesses to prove that Johnson had never intended to violate the law or the Constitution. General Sherman was summoned, in addition to Montgomery Meigs, the Army's quartermaster general, and others. The trial managers were able to delay the testimony of General Sherman, who did not appear until April 13. Sherman's words were compelling. He stated that "Johnson's intent had been to have the office [of the secretary of war] administered in the interest of the army and the country and that he thought if Stanton's case could be brought before the courts it would not stand half an hour," as noted by historian Trefousse. For the managers, Sherman's testimony was difficult. As some of Johnson's cabinet members testified through the week that followed, Johnson had not intended to break the law.

By the end of April, the main parts of the trial were completed, with the exception of the closing arguments by both the defense team and the board of managers, which would take place in early May. At that point, after weeks of testimony, speeches, and accusations, the defense team was confident of an acquittal. Johnson's lawyers even found themselves laughing together in the White House, in Johnson's presence, about the possibility of conviction. Others felt the same way. By mid-April, Secretary

Welles, who had been certain of Johnson's conviction, stated that impeachment was becoming less likely. According to historian Trefousse, even Benjamin Butler privately "admitted to Evarts that he wished he were on the other side."

Johnson himself was so certain of acquittal that he began taking steps once again to replace Secretary of War Stanton. On the afternoon of April 21, Evarts met with General John Schofield in the Willard Hotel in Washington, asking him to stand for the secretary's position. When Schofield asked General Grant for his permission, Grant, who by then believed the president would survive the trial, agreed. Schofield finally accepted, but only after he received assurances that Johnson would no longer stand in the way of Congress-led Reconstruction. This was not a new promise. Evarts himself had, during the trial, spent considerable time passing along assurances that an acquitted Johnson would not go out of his way again to obstruct radical Reconstruction.

Even as the outcome of the trial seemed secure to many, the final presentations by the managers and the defense team still had to be made. Some of the final speeches were strange in content, such as that of manager George Boutwell, who suggested, according to historian Trefousse, that "Johnson be banished to the black hole in the Southern Sky." Another manager, John Logan, said of the president, as noted by historian Gene Smith:

> The virtues that should adorn a Chief Magistrate fled on the induction of this criminal into that high office. Almost from the time when the blood of Lincoln was warm on the floor of Ford's Theatre, Andrew Johnson was contemplating treason. . . . His great aim and purpose has been to subvert law, usurp authority, insult and outrage Congress, reconstruct the rebel states in the interests of treason, insult the memories and resting places of our heroic dead.

It all seemed too much: too overstated, dramatic, and lacking in fact.

THE SUMMARY ARGUMENTS

Attorney Thomas Nelson presented the defense's closing remarks, stretching into two days. He told the senators and the assembled throng in the gallery that, if Johnson actually was guilty of everything he had been accused of during the Senate trial, then he would indeed be a monster, one deserving of a lashing. Noted by historian Smith, Nelson suggested that "the sight of him would make people's hair stand on end like a porcupine, and his name could be used to frighten naughty children." But was Johnson really as he had been portrayed? The defense attorney reminded the audience that Johnson had spoken in favor of the Union when every other Southern politician seemed to side with the rebels. Johnson had tried to uphold the Constitution, argued Nelson.

Then, William Groesbeck spoke, reminding those listening that much of the case against Johnson was about Stanton and his removal as secretary of war, which had never actually been completed. Groesbeck referred to the Sedition Act of 1798, passed by Federalists in Congress who wanted to protect President Adams from criticism by his political opponents. Such a law was intended to close the mouths of those who believed differently than the president of the United States. Johnson had spoken out critically of Congress, but Groesbeck argued that he should not be punished for his strong convictions.

Then, Groesbeck summed up his presentation, referring to Johnson and his basic character and personality, as noted by historian Gene Smith:

> He is not learned and scholarly, like many of you. He is not a man of many ideas, or of much speculation. But by a law of the mind he is only the truer to that he does know. He is a patriot, second to no one of you in the measure of his patriotism. He may be full of error. I will not canvass now his views. But he loves his country. He has the courage to defend it, and I believe to die for it if need be. His courage and his patriotism are not without illustration. . . . I do hope you will

As chief justice of the U.S. Supreme Court, Salmon P. Chase (above) presided over Andrew Johnson's impeachment hearings in the Senate. Chase, who knew the proceedings would set legal precedents for future cases, was determined to establish a dignified, impartial trial that would focus solely on Johnson's violations of the Tenure of Office Act.

not drive the President out and take possession of his office. I hope this not merely as counsel for Andrew Johnson, for Andrew Johnson's Administration is to me but as a moment, and himself as nothing in comparison with the possible consequences of such an act. No good can come of it, Senators.

There were other voices during the days that followed, including Thaddeus Stevens. On the verge of dying, Stevens had to be assisted just to stand while he spoke. Stevens was so weak

A Dying Stevens

At the time of President Johnson's trial, Thaddeus Stevens was in declining health. Although he was chosen as a member of the legal team that was to try Johnson following his impeachment, he was unable to take an active role during the days of testimony. He sat quietly, wrapped in a blanket, raising his head occasionally to whisper counsel in the ears of his colleagues whose task it was to prosecute Johnson. Then, on Monday, April 27, after the trial had dragged on for nearly two months, the frail congressman rose to speak.

The scene would prove to be one of the most dramatic of the trial. Stevens was so frail he had to be carried into the Senate Chamber by a pair of black servants, who propped him up. He accused Johnson of betrayal, of committing high crimes and misdemeanors. Johnson had taken the oath of office, said Stevens, with no intention of upholding all the laws of the land—just those with which he agreed.

Then, Stevens could no longer stand, and he requested permission to continue speaking while sitting down. He continued slowly, his voice growing weaker. He expressed sorrow for the day that Johnson had become president. Then, he launched into a political speech, claiming that Congress should have had the responsibility of Reconstruction, a task that Johnson had attempted to take over for himself. Johnson must be stopped, said Stevens; the Senate must find him guilty.

At that point, Stevens's voice finally gave out. Benjamin Butler stepped forward to continue the speech, reading Stevens's words loudly to those assembled. Stevens was shrouded in blankets, tired from his struggle to continue his long fight, one that had preoccupied him as a national leader for decades. His words would continue as Butler read on, but he was a finished man. A disappointed Stevens lived to see Johnson's acquittal, remaining alive through the summer of 1868 and dying on August 11.

His old colleague in the Senate, Charles Sumner, delivered Stevens's eulogy. He spoke glowingly of Stevens's long career and of his constant support of black equality.

he could not finish his speech, but he allowed Butler to read it for him.

Defense attorney Evarts followed Butler. Evarts drove home his point that Johnson was on trial, largely, for firing a member of his cabinet. As Gene Smith notes, Evarts stated: "And what exactly had the President done? What, precisely, was his crime? He had removed a member of the Cabinet. That was hardly an unprecedented occurrence, still less an act of terror. It could hardly be termed total depravity." As had Groesbeck, Evarts referred to Johnson's simple patriotism and his love of the Constitution: "He is no rhetorician and no theorist, no sophist and no philosopher. The Constitution is to him the only political book that he reads. To the Constitution he adheres."

The final voices of the trial were Stanbery for the defense and Bingham for the prosecution. Stanbery had become quite ill early during the trial, but he took his turn, speaking of Johnson as an old friend. Historian Smith recalls his speech: "Yes, Senators, with all his faults, the President has been more sinned against than sinning. Fear not, then, to acquit him. The Constitution of the country is as safe in his hands from violence as it was in the hands of [President] Washington." When Bingham spoke, he simply repeated the sentiments, concerns, and condemnations that already had been expressed. It was May 7, and the trial of Andrew Johnson was nearly over.

Salmon Chase then stated that the Senate could vote within the next five days. On May 12, a senator from Michigan turned up sick and could not attend. The vote was such an important one that the Senate delayed its decision until Saturday, May 16. At noon that day, Chief Justice Chase stepped onto the Senate floor and took his seat. The House members, the board of managers, and Johnson's defense counsel filed in 15 minutes later. The session was called to order. A senator moved that the vote be taken on the eleventh charge first, and the motion was carried almost immediately. As that vote was taken, the sena-

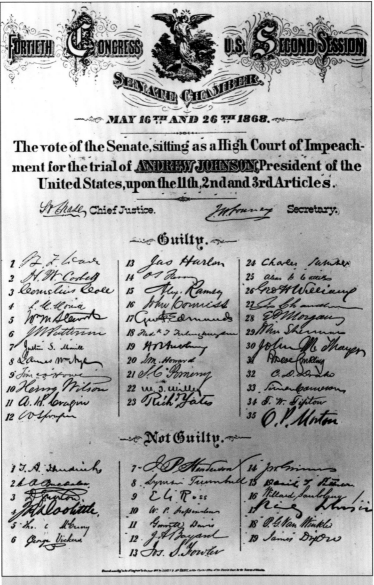

The Republican Party ultimately was not united enough to remove the president from office. A few senators broke party lines and voted against impeaching the president, which prevented the Senate from acquiring the two-thirds majority necessary to push Johnson out of the presidency. Above, the final vote of the Senate displaying the signatures of those who were for or against impeachment.

tor who had been ill earlier in the week was brought in, barely able to walk. Then another senator who had recently suffered a stroke was delivered into the chamber.

Chase ordered those in the gallery to remain silent and then called for the vote. Johnson's political and personal future would soon be decided. The roll was taken alphabetically, starting with Senator Henry B. Anthony, who voted against Johnson. Most of the votes were cast along party lines, with the Democrats and conservatives voting "not guilty." Republicans voted to convict the president, but the party wall against Johnson was not solid. Seven Republicans—William Pitt Fessenden, Joseph Fowler, James Grimes, John B. Henderson, Edmund G. Ross, Lyman Trumbull, and Peter G. Van Winkle—broke with their party and cast votes in favor of Johnson.

The vote could not have been closer. The final tally included 35 in favor of convicting Johnson and 19 against. By a single vote, Johnson had avoided removal from office. Edmund Ross cast the deciding vote. Although there were votes following his alphabetically, the result of the vote was already known. The Radical Republicans had failed to remove President Johnson from office.

Reconstruction and Black Gains

In the aftermath of the failed attempt by the Radical Republicans to remove President Johnson from office, the direction of Reconstruction continued, largely without further interruptions from the president. The impeachment and the trial had taught Johnson a lesson. He had survived to hold on to his presidency, but he would rarely challenge the course of radical Reconstruction. Congress was relatively free to continue its intentions to bring equality and the vote to the nation's freedmen. As for the seven Republicans who had voted for Johnson's acquittal, none were reelected to their office.

RECONSTRUCTION CONTINUES

Even during the impeachment and trial, progress had continued on Reconstruction, especially for Southern blacks. Blacks were selected as delegates to various constitutional conventions in former Confederate states, with the notable exception of Tennessee, which already had been restored back into the

United States. Some Southern whites refused to participate in these conventions. As a result, many delegates were either Republicans or conservative Southern Democrats.

Among the Republicans attending such conventions, there were three groups: the carpetbaggers, those white Northerners who had moved into the South to take advantage of the economic and political possibilities after the war; white Southerners, often referred to as "scalawags," many of whom were small-time farmers who thought they might gain by allying with the Republicans; and Southern blacks. Of the 1,000 delegates selected to attend 10 state conventions, 265 were black. The majority—158 out of 265—had never been slaves, and about 1 out of 6 had served in the Union Army during the war. In two states, Louisiana and South Carolina, blacks made up a majority. In most, they represented between 10 and 20 percent.

With blacks included in the state constitutional conventions, new gains were soon made for Southern freedmen. These new constitutions allowed for all adult males to vote, regardless of race, and they also included guarantees of civil rights. In addition, most of these constitutions established public schools for all Southern children. Previous generations had denied black children access to reading and writing, and the new constitutions intended to open up the schoolhouse door to them.

Before the end of the year, elections were held across the South to ratify the new constitutions and to elect new state officials. Most of these constitutions did not take away the vote from those who had fought for or otherwise supported the Confederacy. Even so, in some states, some whites boycotted these elections, protesting black candidates and black voting. This move was not in their own best interests, since it allowed an even greater number of blacks to be elected. Ratification of the new constitutions only required a majority vote of those who actually cast their ballots, not a majority of all registered voters.

BLACK EMPOWERMENT

A new day had dawned for the black man across the South. Between 1868 and the late 1870s, nearly 1,500 black men were elected to Southern offices, including to the U.S. Congress. For the most part, the number of elected black officials paralleled the size of a given state's black population. Mississippi, Louisiana, and South Carolina, where blacks were a majority of the population, were the states to elect the largest percentage of black officials. During the 1868 elections, blacks largely ran for offices other than Congress, concerned they would antagonize whites further by being elected to the national legislature. But by 1870, after white Republicans had been elected in large numbers, blacks ran for every possible office.

The results produced a wave of black office holders. Although no black governors were elected, 2 black candidates, Blanche K. Bruce and Hiram Revels, were elected as Mississippi's 2 new U.S. senators. From 1870 until the official end of Reconstruction (1877), Southerners elected 14 blacks to the U.S. House of Representatives; 6 blacks served as state lieutenant governors. In several states, blacks dominated the membership of state legislatures, and black legislators served as speakers of the house in 2 of them. During the last 7 years of Reconstruction, nearly 800 black politicians served in their state legislatures. A black state supreme court justice was chosen in South Carolina. There were black state superintendents of education, a secretary of state, a state treasurer, 41 sheriffs, 5 mayors, and 31 state coroners. In Tallahassee and Little Rock, citizens elected black chiefs of police.

How well qualified were these black political winners during the late years of Reconstruction? The legacy is mixed. The majority were well-qualified men, some with college degrees, political experience, or other backgrounds that prepared them for their new political roles. Looking at the total number of 1,465 black office holders, about one-quarter were free men before the opening of the Civil War. Statistics show that 933 were

While the Senate was immersed in impeachment proceedings, advancements in Reconstruction continued throughout the South. Dramatic changes came in the forms of public schools, Freedmen's Bureaus, and the passing of the Civil Rights Acts of 1866 and 1875. Granted the right to vote, black men rushed to the polls and ushered almost 1,500 black officials into public office. One of these men, Hiram R. Revels (above), became the first black U.S. senator in 1870.

literate and 195 were illiterate. (As to the remaining 337, there is no record of their literacy.) There were 64 who had college or professional school degrees, 14 of whom had attended the same institution, Oberlin College in Ohio. Others included businessmen, ministers, farmers, professional artisans and craftsmen, teachers, and Army veterans.

The new black office holders soon became part of a larger political landscape of U.S. government. It is not possible to state that all black politicians supported the same political agenda. Still, there were several key issues they did tend to support with large majorities. Nearly all black and white Republicans during the 1870s supported the idea that state governments should be used to see to the welfare of their citizens by providing public schools, medical care, and other social services.

Schools were a key to the Republican program. Black political leaders wanted to see educational opportunities for people of their race. Some schools were built, but many Southern rural areas continued to do without a local school for many years. In some cases and places, black Reconstruction leaders helped establish, through the 1862 Morrill Land-Grant Act, black colleges. They also encouraged traditionally white educational systems, such as the University of South Carolina, to allow blacks to attend. When the university did enroll black students and hire black faculty, however, many white students left, along with several white faculty.

RIGHTS AND OPPORTUNITIES

Another important issue to the black political leaders was civil rights. It was ironic that, even as black men were being elected to state legislatures and to the U.S. Congress, they also experienced ongoing racism that might deny them the use of public transportation, a night's stay in a hotel or inn, or a meal in a restaurant. Such officials often set a course for desegregation, opening up public facilities and accommodations to blacks.

Southern state legislatures soon saw bills introduced to require those operating such venues as restaurants, taverns, inns, streetcars, concert halls and auditoriums, and steamboats and ferries to no longer exclude black customers' access. In most instances, white politicians kept most such bills from passing. South Carolina was the exception, with a black majority in its house and many others in its senate. Still, even the law passed there was not commonly enforced. In some states, bills were passed that actually supported segregation.

Another issue supported by the new black legislators and state officials focused on increased economic opportunities for blacks. For example, some Southern white landowners employed black workers through a growing season, and then fired them before the laborers received their pay at harvest. To remedy this practice, laws were passed requiring landowners to pay wages to workers before a crop was sold. "Stay laws" were passed to protect both black and white small landowners from having their property instantly taken for not paying debts. (Republicans supported such laws often because they hoped poorer farmers would abandon the Democratic Party and support them instead.)

Another economic issue was land reform. Black politicians tried to get laws passed that would provide land for those people, black and white, who needed land that was usually distributed by the state. In nearly every case, such bills did not pass. Again, only in South Carolina was a land commission established, in 1869, to purchase and distribute land to the state's freedmen. In all, the commission helped 14,000 black families, as well as a small number of whites, to purchase property from the state.

On another economic front, black lawmakers tried to encourage the expansion of their state's economic investment in business and industry. One target was railroad expansion, which was popular among Republicans of every race everywhere. States supported bond sales to finance railroad construction, especially in Georgia, Alabama, Arkansas, and Texas. Blacks also supported the formation of corporations that provided money to establish new businesses, factories, mills, and railroads. They even helped establish horse streetcar lines, such as the one in Charleston, which was financed by a group of 28 prominent black leaders and politicians.

Overall, the new black political leaders helped bring improvements to the lives of people of color across the South. They helped establish public school systems and encourage education for blacks. They worked in support of special schools for the blind, deaf, and those with mental illnesses. Their efforts to pass laws against segregation met stiff objection, but their efforts did succeed occasionally. Black leaders also helped expand the economic bases in their states. Party Republicans, black and white, were behind nearly all of this effort.

Across the South, Republicans and blacks were working together against the traditional political power of white Democrats. This new political reality caused significant frictions between the two parties, between the races, and between Southern whites and Northern carpetbaggers. Conservative white Southerners could hardly tolerate the idea, much less the reality, of black men holding public office. They despised Northerners on their soil, those "carpetbaggers" whom most Southerners thought of as vultures looking for any opportunity. Historian Darlene Hine refers to a white man from Florida who spoke bitterly about the new politics of the post–Civil War era: "The damned Republican Party has put niggers to rule us and we will not suffer it." In most Southern states, however, black politicians hardly ruled at all. White Southerners usually missed that point, and they had an equal distain for black politicians and the Republican Party.

NEW PRESIDENT, NEW LEGISLATION

As President Johnson rode out the final months of his presidency in 1868, the Republicans geared up to elect a new president, General Ulysses S. Grant. On the other side, the Democrats met in a convention on Independence Day in New York City during days of terrible summer heat. They selected New York governor Horatio Seymour, who was chosen on the twenty-second ballot from a field of nearly four-dozen candidates. Although Seymour was a reluctant nominee, party leaders spoke out loud and clear in opposition to Republican Reconstruction policies.

Johnson continued to block the ratification of the Fourteenth Amendment, but he failed. It became law by late July. By that time, seven former Confederate states had been readmitted to the Union, six alone within a four-day period in June. This left only Virginia, Mississippi, Texas, and Georgia yet to be readmitted under Congress's Reconstruction plan.

The campaign proved uneventful, with nearly everyone certain of Grant's election. Grant said little during the campaign, but he was often quoted for the same line: "Let us have peace." That November, Grant was elected by only 300,000 popular votes over Seymour, much to the surprise of many, yet the electoral college vote was much wider, 214 to 80. Some of Grant's most significant support came from Southern blacks. The freedmen's vote, which accounted for 450,000 votes cast, made all the difference in Grant's election.

Following the election, President Johnson kept up his practice of blocking actions with which he disagreed. He even vetoed bills that would have brought additional states back into the Union, certain still that the radical Reconstruction plan was unconstitutional. As noted by historians Jacobs and Robinson, Johnson delivered his final address to Congress, and in it he blamed violence by the Ku Klux Klan on "the attempt to place the white population under the domination of persons of color." Through four years as president, Johnson had managed to veto 22 bills, most related to Reconstruction.

The day of the inauguration, on March 4 in those days, Grant was so disgusted with Johnson that he refused to ride with him in the same carriage. In fact, Johnson chose to skip the inauguration altogether, taking care of some last-minute business that day and leaving the White House quietly and unseen.

General Ulysses S. Grant sided with the Republican Party during Johnson's impeachment hearings, and the Republicans returned the favor by nominating him as their presidential candidate in 1868. Above, the national Republican nomination for Grant and his vice president, Schuyler Colfax, in the 1868 election.

It was a manner quite different from the one he had during his controversial presidency. As Grant spoke to the nation that day, among other things, he gave his support to the ratification of the Fifteenth Amendment, which had just passed through Congress in February.

Over the next few years, Congress and the president worked much closer together than they had in years. During Grant's first year as president, the Fifteenth Amendment, the third of the Reconstruction amendments, moved through the

White Supremacy Organizes:
The Ku Klux Klan

The vast changes that resulted from the Civil War, especially those that brought blacks new social and political power, caused many Southerners to feel pressures they had never faced before. This mindset gave rise to militant organizations across the South, including the Knights of the White Camellia, the White Brotherhood, the Whitecaps, and, most famous, the Ku Klux Klan.

The Ku Klux Klan was first established in Pulaski, Tennessee, in 1866. Originally, the Klan was little more than a social club for former Confederate veterans, especially officers. One of its founders, the organization's original Grand Wizard, was former general Nathan Bedford Forrest from Mississippi, who had been a successful Confederate cavalry commander in Tennessee. The Klan's original members met as a fraternal organization, wearing costumes that "disguised" the wearers, and engaged in secret oaths and rituals.

Soon, however, Forrest began to direct the Klan's efforts against Southern Republicans. Other separate "Klan" groups were formed, having no actual ties to or direction from Forrest. These groups began to engage in intimidation of blacks. By 1867, Klan chapters had been established in nine Southern states, with the exceptions of Virginia and Louisiana, where its membership was either small or nonexistent.

Historians Jacobs and Robinson quoted one expert in the methods of the group as saying that the Klan "threatened, exiled, flogged, mutilated, shot, stabbed, and hanged to gain its

states, only to be ratified the following year (March 1870). The amendment required that no person be deprived of his right to vote on the basis of race. The wording of the amendment seemed clear: "The right of citizens of the United States to vote shall not be denied or abridged by the United States or by any State on account of race, color, or previous condition of servitude."

ends." Black churches and schools were burned. A black leader in the Republican Party in South Carolina was murdered while leaving a train in 1868. Other black officials and political leaders were killed. A white senator in North Carolina was murdered for being a Republican. In 1869, Klansmen beat a former Alabama slave who voted Republican, and they also raped a young woman who only happened to be in the victim's house visiting his wife. In the face of such terror tactics, black victims had little power to oppose.

The Klan did not reserve all its hatred for the black population. Whites also were targeted, including influential and wealthy white supporters of the Republican Party. Those who cooperated with Republicans or helped blacks in even the slightest way might receive a death threat. A newly elected white governor of Louisiana received one in 1868, as quoted by historian Richard Current: "Villain, beware. Your doom is sealed. *Death* now awaits you. The midnight owl screams: Revenge! Revenge!! Revenge!!! *Ku Klux Klan.*"

As their tactics became bolder and more terrorizing, public sentiment turned on the Klan. Even General Forrest called for the dissolving of all Klan chapters by 1869. In 1870 and 1871, Republicans in Congress passed the Enforcement Acts (popularly known as the Ku Klux Klan Act), which not only intended to protect the civil rights of the Klan's victims, but outlawed the hoods and masks used by the Klan. The organization declined between 1868 and 1870 and was nearly destroyed by President Grant's enforcement of the Civil Rights Act of 1871.

Before the end of the 1870s, the Klan was dead, but a new Klan would be organized nearly 50 years later, in 1915, and another wave of organized, hooded white supremacy began in U.S. history.

To many supporters of black equality, the amendment signaled the end of a long national campaign, not only to end slavery, but also to guarantee the rights and privileges of blacks on an equal basis with whites. The amendment would have an impact on the North as well as the South. At its ratification, blacks were only allowed to vote in 8 of the 22 Northern states.

Events began to turn quickly for Reconstruction during the Grant years. The three-way power share of Southern politics held among the carpetbaggers, scalawags, and Southern blacks would not last forever. By 1872, when Grant was up for reelection, four Southern states that had successfully completed Reconstruction had come under the control of white Southerners, often called "Redeemers," once again. Several factors account for this shift in power back to its traditional base. One primary influence was the militant terror tactics of the Ku Klux Klan and other such groups across the South. By sheer intimidation and even murder, the Klan had frightened black and white Republican voters from going to the polls. This was the case despite a specific act of Congress to limit the effectiveness of the Klan.

THE KU KLUX KLAN ACT

In 1870, Congress passed the first of two "enforcement" acts. The First Enforcement Act made illegal the cloaks, white costumes, hoods, and masks worn by Ku Klux Klan members, all designed to protect each member's identity. The Second Enforcement Act, passed in February 1871, provided for federal supervisors to monitor elections across the South.

But, even when the two acts became law, the efforts of the Ku Klux Klan and other militant groups continued. This prompted President Grant to call an early session of Congress following the November 1870 elections. By March 1871, Congress had passed the Third Enforcement Act, commonly known as the Ku Klux Klan Act. This act made it a federal crime to stop someone from voting, holding office, serving on a jury, or

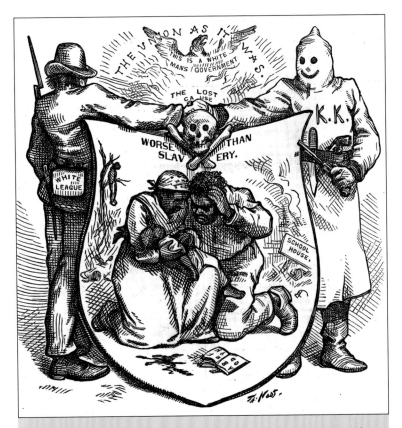

As Reconstruction progressed, militant organizations like the Ku Klux Klan emerged and spread throughout the South. Members of these groups engaged in acts of terror to intimidate blacks and white Republicans. In response, Congress passed three Enforcement Acts in an attempt to halt further violence. Above, an illustration depicting the united efforts of the White League and the Ku Klux Klan in restoring a white government by terrorizing black families.

denying them any other right common to U.S. citizens, since everyone was provided equal protection under the law. In extreme examples of any of these, the act authorized the president of the United States to dispatch federal troops to stop whatever organized or large-scale harassment was taking place. Black politicians en masse supported the Enforcement Acts.

Grant was quick to present these new laws to the American people, expressing the need to enforce them, according to historians Jacobs and Robinson, "in certain localities lately the theater of insurrection." In reality, though, the enforcement laws were not often enforced. The truth was that many Americans across the North already were growing tired of Reconstruction.

The acts helped to limit Klan activity for a time, but white Southerners in general had never been convinced that blacks should hold any political power in the South. They thought, instead, that white supremacy must be reestablished. Blacks continued to be harassed and intimidated by Klan violence, even as the level dropped off in the long run and the Klan ultimately declined in significance during the early 1870s. Even after 1870, fewer numbers of blacks were still voting in elections. In 1875, in one largely black county in Mississippi, only 7 blacks voted. That year, 150 blacks were victims of violence in Mississippi, yet, when protests and appeals were made to President Grant, he did little. According to historians Jacobs and Robinson, Grant's own attorney general said: "The whole public are tired of the annual autumnal outbreaks in the south."

TIRED OF RECONSTRUCTION

By the mid-1870s, then, Reconstruction had become unpleasant not only for Southerners, but even for Northerners. Then, new legal interpretations of laws passed during Reconstruction changed their original intention and ultimate impact. The U.S. Supreme Court, in 1875, issued a ruling in the case *United States v. Cruikshank*, in which the highest court in the land determined that the Fifteenth Amendment did not necessarily guarantee a black man's right to vote. Instead, the court stated, the amendment "merely prevented race being used as a standard or test for voting," explain historians Jacobs and Robinson.

It also was becoming clearer to Southerners that Northerners had never truly been committed to upholding their own expectations of Reconstruction. Northern politicians had forced Southerners to provide the vote to blacks while most Northern states themselves did not allow black suffrage. In Pennsylvania, radical Republican Thaddeus Stevens's own home state, transportation systems were not desegregated until 1867. The state's school system did not integrate until 1881, four years after the end of Reconstruction. Equality for blacks was no more a goal in the Northern states than it had been among white Southerners.

Some critics of Reconstruction, both North and South, became convinced that Republicans had supported black voting rights only to ensure that blacks would vote for members of their party. As Jacobs and Robinson noted, one Southerner, Albion Tourgee, wrote that Northerners had taken political advantage of Southern blacks, and then they grew tired of the ongoing responsibility of protecting them. The North then, Tourgee wrote, came to believe it "could at any time unload him upon the states where he chanced to dwell, wash its hands of all further responsibility in the matter, and leave him to live or die as chance might determine."

Southern Democrats took advantage of the new situation and worked hard to rally as many white voters as possible and elect as many white leaders as possible, while restricting as many black votes as possible. Beginning in 1872 and continuing on the same path over the following four years, white Southern Democrats made inroads, sometimes continuing to rely on violence against blacks, certain that the federal government would do little to stop them.

Other problems began to preoccupy Northerners, including political corruption within the Grant administration, as well as a poor economy (the country experienced a serious economic downturn in 1873). By the election of 1876, Reconstruction was about to collapse. As historian David Goldfield puts it: "Reconstruction did not end; it was overthrown."

A Failed Legacy

With declining Northern commitment to continue Reconstruction, Southern Democrats moved to gain former political ground they had lost during previous years. With no expectation that Northern authorities would try and stop them, these Southerners largely relied on corruption, intimidation, and violence, just as the Klan had earlier. These white men of the South who sought to restore the power of white supremacy and of the Democratic Party sometimes referred to their actions as "Redemption" and saw themselves as "Redeemers." As historian Goldfield describes them, they believed they were "holy warriors who had saved the South from the hell of black Republican rule."

TAKING CONTROL OF RECONSTRUCTION

Between 1874 and 1876, the "Redeemers" pursued their goals, not under cover of darkness under bed sheets as the Klan had, but in the naked light of day. White Democrats marched in campaign rallies, flanked by former Confederates in their old gray uniforms. They publicly scolded blacks for trying to bring about change and discouraged them from voting. Many blacks responded with fear and stayed away from the polls.

The 1874 elections across the South represented Democrat victories. Not only did blacks not vote, but whites turned out by the battalion, unseating Republicans in Virginia, Florida, and Arkansas. Texas already had gone Democrat in the 1873 elections. In states where black majorities still could have influence, including South Carolina, Mississippi, and Louisiana, the gains by Democrats were limited. But the redirection of Southern politics back to earlier times was clear.

In Louisiana, political change was ushered in through near revolution. Democrats formed a military organization in New Orleans in 1874 called the White League. That fall, 8,000 White League members tried to overthrow the city's Republican-controlled government. They nearly succeeded, except for the intervention of the city police force, led by former Confederate General James Longstreet, who had served directly under Robert E. Lee. Federal troops also helped put down the rebellion.

Despite such unrest and gathering of political power by Southern Democrats, the U.S. Congress still tried to continue Reconstruction with the passage of the Civil Rights Act of 1875. The new federal law further guaranteed the rights of black Americans to have access to public accommodations, including parks, theaters, and transportation, while also reminding people of the right of blacks to serve on juries. With the Fifteenth Amendment in place, the new act stated nothing about guaranteeing voting rights.

With Reconstruction dying in the South, enforcement of such a law was difficult. In nearly every situation, blacks who tried, for example, to use public accommodations, were denied access. In fact, by 1883, the U.S. Supreme Court decided the 1875 act was unconstitutional, stating that only the states had the power to declare such laws, not Congress.

THE END OF RECONSTRUCTION

By 1876, nearly everyone, North and South—with the exception of blacks concerned about the redirecting of Southern
governments by unsympathetic white Southerners—was tired
of Reconstruction. The Civil War had lasted 4 years of direct
fighting, but Reconstruction had dragged on for 12 to 14 years.
For many, enough was enough.

From 1872 and for the four years that followed, Reconstruction shrank, but it did not come to an official end until the
presidential election of 1876. That year, a New York Democrat
named Samuel J. Tilden ran for the presidency against Republican Rutherford B. Hayes. (President Grant had been open to a
third term as president, but some groups within the Republican
Party blocked his nomination.) Throughout the campaign, the
Republicans continued to rally around their legacy of restoring the Union through war. They reminded voters that even
12 years after the end of the Civil War, Democrats had been
the party of secession and rebellion. This was a political tactic
known as "waving the bloody shirt." For the most part, however,
Republicans ignored their legacy of Reconstruction.

Democrats were hopeful that year, given the scandals rock-
ing the Grant administration and the relative weariness of many
with Reconstruction. White Southerners, nearly all Democrats,
hoped to use their political gains made over the previous four
or five years to end the Republican domination of the White
House that had taken place over the previous 16 years. A small
economic depression also looked to give Democrats a boost in
the election, as well.

The ballots were counted following the November vote,
and tallies indicated the Democrat candidate Tilden had, indeed, won. But, although Tilden had received a majority of the
popular vote (4,288,000 vs. 4,034,000 for Hayes), the Democrat
had not taken enough electoral votes to win. With 185 electoral
votes needed, Tilden had polled 184 to Hayes's 165. There were

Rutherford B. Hayes (above), a Civil War veteran and experienced politician, was the Republican nominee for the 1876 presidential election. Though he did not believe he would win against New York Governor Samuel J. Tilden, Hayes eked out a victory by one vote in the electoral college.

20 other electoral votes in dispute, including a vote from Oregon, along with those of three Southern states—Florida, South Carolina, and Louisiana. All three of those Southern states were still operating with Republican-controlled state governments. Tilden only needed 1 of these votes while Hayes needed all 20. Oregon was settled quickly, with its vote going to Hayes. During the months following the election, the Republicans and Democrats both tried to position themselves for a legitimate claim to the 19 remaining electoral votes. In all three cases, dual sets of ballots were submitted to Congress, each claiming a winner in either Tilden or Hayes.

With no clear way to determine which ballots were real, Congress established a 15-member election commission to settle the question. With a Republican-controlled Congress, the membership of the commission ultimately included 7 Democrats and 8 Republicans. In the end, the commission granted the remaining 19 electoral votes to the Republican Hayes, deciding the controversial and bitter election.

But the Democrats were not willing to simply roll over and allow the Republicans to manipulate the political system for their advantage. Ultimately, Democrats cared more about Reconstruction ending and the return of home rule to the Southern states than about who sat in the White House. According to historian David Goldfield, one newspaper editorial summed up the political equation clearly: "It matters little to us who rules in Washington, if South Carolina is allowed to have [Democratic governor Wade] Hampton and Home Rule." For his part, Hayes promised, if elected, to bring Reconstruction to an end immediately. Republicans otherwise made promises to the Democratic South to help build up the Southern economy and to support railroad construction across the region.

The result was the Compromise of 1877, which carried Hayes into office, ended Reconstruction, and paved the way for Democratic control of all the state governments of the former Confederacy. For the most part, the economic promises made

Reconstruction ended with the Compromise of 1877 and ushered in a new era in the South known as Jim Crow. During this time, much of the progress achieved through Reconstruction ended as new laws restricted the civil rights of blacks for decades. Above, a political cartoon illustrating the hypocrisy of requiring blacks to be educated before allowing them to vote.

by Congress as part of the "deal" never occurred, but the South did not care much. Reconstruction was over, and Democratic "Redeemers" were back in power.

Across the South, the impact of the shift in power was clear. Black Southern leaders and office holders would soon be swept out of office in future elections. Southerners would defy the intent of Reconstruction, as it related to empowering blacks and giving support to their equality. Piece by piece, the elements protecting blacks were taken apart, as African Americans were denied their right to vote by backdoor restrictions that included such things as poll taxes, which many blacks could not afford to pay.

THE LEGACY OF RECONSTRUCTION

After at least 12 years, what had Reconstruction accomplished? Radical Republicans had pursued goals that were designed to punish Confederates and those who had sympathized with them, while simultaneously elevating the freedmen to a status equal to any white man. Republicans had been so intent in their efforts to help make a fresh start for blacks across the South that they brought change to the fabric of the U.S. Constitution by supporting the ratification of three amendments. They had created the Freedmen's Bureau in 1865 and the Civil Rights Acts of 1866 and 1875. Those in Congress had challenged the executive branch itself when the president seemed prepared to stand in the way of Republican Reconstruction efforts, even to the point of impeachment and trial. Improvement was made in the lives of many American blacks through such efforts.

But, in the end, Northern Republicans and their counterparts in the South could not maintain a consistent level of commitment to Reconstruction. After years of forward movement on behalf of the freedmen, they began to allow white Southerners to take control and turn some of these successes into ultimate failures.

The Compromise of 1877 reveals this very turn in commitment by the Republicans. The compromise meant a revoking of civil rights for blacks and a denying of their right to vote. The well-intended Fourteenth and Fifteenth Amendments became dead ends, obstacles for white Southerners to skirt around through methods, policies, and practices. Through Jim Crow laws and other segregationist policies, blacks would find themselves engaged in a constant and uphill battle through the remainder of the nineteenth and much of the twentieth century to reestablish gains delivered to them by Reconstruction.

To a great extent, Northerners and Southerners after Reconstruction turned to a new goal: reconciliation. Whites in both national regions finally chose to bury the hatchet and admit that both sides had fought valiantly during the Civil War and that the soldiers of both sides were to be honored. The theme changed from justice to healing. Both goals could have been pursued, but the North chose the one that Southerners ultimately would accept. In the process, blacks came out on the short end. Justice for an entire race of Americans would be postponed until the second half of the twentieth century.

Glossary

ABOLITIONISM   The process of freeing slaves immediately.

ACQUIT   To render a verdict or decision of "not guilty" in a legal case against an accused person.

APPRENTICE   A person who works for someone else for the purpose of learning a skill or trade.

BLACK CODES   Laws passed to limit the personal freedoms of free blacks.

BORDER STATE   A slave state that did not secede from the Union and become a Confederate state. These included Missouri, Kentucky, Maryland, and Delaware.

CARPETBAGGER   Northerners who went South following the Civil War to participate in southern state and local government.

CONFEDERATES OR CONFEDERACY   Those who supported secession from the United States and who fought for the South during the Civil War.

DEMOCRAT PARTY   The political party formed during the age of Andrew Jackson, which supported the Jackson presidency.

EMANCIPATION PROCLAMATION   Official announcement made by President Abraham Lincoln in the fall of 1862 that "freed" all slaves held in states in rebellion against the United States.

ENFRANCHISE   To provide access to voting or other rights of citizenship.

FEDERAL GOVERNMENT   Refers to the national government that holds power by the will of the people. State power is subordinate to federal power.

FIFTEENTH AMENDMENT   Passed by Congress in 1870, this amendment to the Constitution required that no person be deprived of the vote on the basis of race.

FOURTEENTH AMENDMENT   Passed by Congress in 1867, this amendment to the Constitution provided former slaves with their full rights of citizenship.

FREE SOILERS   A political party created during the 1840s and later replaced by the Republican Party. The party did not support the western expansion of slavery.

FREEDMEN   Former slaves who have been granted their freedom.

GANG LABOR   Groups of workers who labor on the same project.

GUERRILLA   An irregular combatant, one who is not part of a regular army as a uniformed soldier.

IMPEACH   To "indict" an official accused of a crime or misdemeanor.

INAUGURATION   Ceremony that includes the swearing-in of a president at the opening of a new four-year term in office.

INDICT   To formally accuse someone of a crime or misdemeanor.

INTEGRATE   To bring together two or more races of people.

INTERNAL IMPROVEMENTS   Building projects that include roads, bridge construction, canals, and railroads.

KANSAS NEBRASKA ACT   An 1854 act of Congress that created the territories of Kansas and Nebraska and opened them up to the potential of slavery.

PARDON   An official set aside of punishment for someone previously found guilty of a crime or unlawful act.

PLANTATION   A large estate, often found in the American South during the eighteenth and early nineteenth centuries, where slavery was typically in practice, usually involving a large number of slaves.

POCKET VETO   A constitutional option which allows the President to kill a bill by merely refusing to sign it.

RATIFICATION   Acceptance of a proposed amendment to the Constitution by two-thirds of the states, making the proposed amendment into law.

RECONSTRUCTION   The restoration of the South into the United States during the years following the Civil War (1865-1877).

REDEEMERS   White southerners who sought to restore their own control over southern politics following the Civil War.

REPUBLICANS   Those holding membership or identity in the Republican Party, which was formed during the early 1850s and was generally a northern party in its base.

SCALAWAG   Name given by white southerners to black leaders and pro-Union whites across the South following the Civil War.

SECEDE   To separate or remove a state from a larger state.

SEGREGATE   To keep two or more races of people separated from one another.

SHARECROPPING   Labor system common to blacks following the Civil War. Workers labor on another's land, with the landowner providing everything needed to farm, including a plow, mule, and seed. The worker "pays back" his debt to the landowner out of his annual harvest.

STATE RIGHTS   The political theory that proposes that the rights of the states comes first over the power of the federal government.

STAY LAWS   Statutes that restrict the potential for one's property to be seized by a creditor for nonpayment of debts.

SUFFRAGE   The right to vote.

SUMMATION   Final remarks made by defense and prosecutors during a trial.

TEN PERCENT PLAN   Lincoln's proposed plan for restoring the Union following the Civil War. The plan allowed a Confederate state to rejoin the U.S. after a number of people equivalent to 10 percent or greater of those voting in the 1860 election pledged loyalty oaths to the federal government.

THIRTEENTH AMENDMENT   Amendment to the U.S. Constitution which brought an official end to slavery in the United States. The amendment was passed by Congress in January 1865 and ratified by the states in December.

UNDERGROUND RAILROAD   A secret system of safe houses for escaped slaves to follow to northern freedom.

"WAVING THE BLOOD SHIRT"   Post-Civil War Republican political tactic of reminding voters that Democrats had been the party of secession and rebellion that had divided the country during the Civil War.

WHIG PARTY   American political party created during the 1830s in response to President Andrew Jackson. The party opposed many of Jackson's political views and remained in existence for about 20 years until the early 1850s. The Republican Party established in the early 1850s included former Whigs.

Bibliography

Basler, Roy P., ed. *The Collected Works of Abraham Lincoln*. Vol. VII and VIII. New Brunswick, NJ: 1953 to 1955.

Belz, Herman. *Reconstructing the Union: Theory and Policy During the Civil War*. New York, NY: Cornell University Press, 1969.

Cox, LaWanda and John H. Cox. *Politics, Principle, and Prejudice, 1865–1866: Dilemma of Reconstruction America*. New York, NY: Free Press, 1963.

Current, Richard Nelson. *Those Terrible Carpetbaggers: A Reinterpretation*. New York, NY: Oxford University Press, 1988.

Foner, Eric. *Reconstruction: America's Unfinished Revolution, 1863–1877*. New York, NY: Harper & Row, 1988.

Franklin, John Hope. *Reconstruction After the Civil War*. Chicago, IL: University of Chicago Press, 1961.

Goldfield, David R., et al. *The American Journey: A History of the United States*. Upper Saddle River, NJ: Pearson Prentice Hall, 2004.

Goodwin, Doris Kearns. *Team of Rivals: The Political Genius of Abraham Lincoln*. New York, NY: Simon & Schuster, 2005.

Hine, Darlene Clark, et al. *The African-American Odyssey*. Upper Saddle River, NJ: Prentice Hall, 2000.

Horton, James Oliver and Louis E. Horton. *Slavery and the Making of America*. New York, NY: Oxford University Press, 2005.

Hyman, Harold M., ed. *The Radical Republicans and Reconstruction, 1861–1870*. Indianapolis, IN: The Bobbs-Merrill Company, 1967.

Jacobs, Donald M. and Raymond H. Robinson. *America's Testing Time, 1848–1877*. Boston, MA: Allyn and Bacon, 1973.

Kauffman, Michael. *American Brutus: John Wilkes Booth and the Lincoln Conspiracies*. New York, NY: Random House, 2004.

McKitrick, Eric L. *Andrew Johnson and Reconstruction*. Chicago, IL: University of Chicago Press, 1960.

McPherson, James. *Ordeal by Fire: The Civil War and Reconstruction.* New York, NY: McGraw-Hill, 1991.

Morris, Roy Jr. *Fraud of the Century: Rutherford B. Hayes, Samuel Tilden and the Stolen Election of 1876.* New York, NY: Simon and Schuster, 2003.

Shenton, James P., ed. *The Reconstruction: A Documentary History of the South After the War: 1865–1877.* New York, NY: G.P. Putnam's Sons, 1963.

Smith, Gene. *High Crimes and Misdemeanors: The Impeachment and Trial of Andrew Johnson.* New York, NY: William Morrow and Company, 1977.

Swanson, James L. *Manhunt: The 12-Day Chase for Lincoln's Killer.* New York, NY: HarperCollins, 2006.

Trefousse, Hans L. *Andrew Johnson: A Biography.* New York, NY: W.W. Norton & Company, 1989.

Vaughan, William P. *Schools for All: The Blacks and Public Education in the South, 1865–1877.* Lexington, KY: University of Kentucky Press, 1974.

"Wade-Davis Manifesto." *New York Tribune,* August 5, 1864.

Ward, Geoffrey. *The Civil War: An Illustrated History.* New York, NY: Knopf, 1990.

Weinstein, Allen and David Rubel. *The Story of America: Freedom and Crisis From Settlement to Superpower.* New York, NY: DK Publishing, 2002.

Woodburn, James Albert. *The Life of Thaddeus Stevens: A Study in American Political History, Especially in the Period of the Civil War and Reconstruction.* 1913. Available online. URL: http://www.questia.com/PM.qst?a=o&d=3161778.

Further Resources

Barney, William L. *Civil War and Reconstruction: A Student Companion*. New York, NY: Oxford University Press, 2001.

King, David C. *Civil War and Reconstruction*. Hoboken, NJ: John Wiley & Sons, 2003.

Matuz, Roger. *Reconstruction Era*. San Diego, CA: Gale Research, 2004.

Stanley, George Edward. *Era of Reconstruction and Expansion, 1865–1900*. Strongsville, OH: Gareth Stevens Publishing, 2005.

Stroud, Bettye and Virginia Schomp. *The Reconstruction Era*. Tarrytown, NY: Marshall Cavendish, 2006.

WEB SITES

America's Reconstruction: People and Politics After the Civil War
http://www.digitalhistory.uh.edu/reconstruction/index.html

Reconstruction on About.com
http://afroamhistory.about.com/od/reconstruction/Reconstruction.htm

American Experience: Reconstruction, The Second Civil War
http://www.pbs.org/wgbh/amex/reconstruction

Reconstruction Era on About.com
http://americanhistory.about.com/od/reconstruction/Reconstruction_
Era.htm

American Civil War Reconstruction Era and Acts: 1865–1877
http://thomaslegion.net/reconstruction.html

The Impeachment of Andrew Johnson
http://www.andrewjohnson.com

Biography of Andrew Johnson
http://www.whitehouse.gov/history/presidents/aj17.html

Andrew Johnson
http://statelibrary.dcr.state.nc.us/nc/bio/public/johnson.htm

Picture Credits

Index

About
the Author

TIM McNEESE is associate professor of history at York College in York, Nebraska, where he is in his seventeenth year of college instruction. Professor McNeese earned an associate of arts degree from York College, a bachelor of arts in history and political science from Harding University, and a master of arts in history from Missouri State University. A prolific author of books for elementary, middle, and high school, and college readers, McNeese has published more than 100 books and educational materials over the past 20 years, on everything from the founding of early New York to Hispanic authors. His writing has earned him a citation in the library reference work *Contemporary Authors* and multiple citations in *Best Books for Young Teen Readers*. In 2006, McNeese appeared on the History Channel program *Risk Takers, History Makers: John Wesley Powell and the Grand Canyon*. He was a faculty member at the 2006 Tony Hillerman Writers Conference in Albuquerque. His wife, Beverly, is an assistant professor of English at York College. They have two married children, Noah and Summer, and three grandchildren, Ethan, Adrianna, and Finn William. Tim and Bev McNeese sponsored study trips for college students on the Lewis and Clark Trail in 2003 and 2005 and to the American Southwest in 2008. You may contact Professor McNeese at tdmcneese@york.edu.

Lake Oswego Jr. High
2500 SW Country Club Rd.
Lake Oswego, OR 97034
503-534-2335